LOST RAI
OF
DORSET

Leslie Oppitz

COUNTRYSIDE BOOKS

NEWBURY, BERKSHIRE

COUNTRYSIDE BOOKS
3 Catherine Road
Newbury, Berkshire

To view our complete range of books,
please visit us at
www.countrysidebooks.co.uk

ISBN 978 1 85306 696 2

The cover picture shows West Country Class locomotive 34106
'Lydford' passing through Christchurch station, with a non-stop
Waterloo-Bournemouth express on 8th April, 1955.
(From an original painting by Colin Doggett)

Produced through The Letterworks Ltd., Reading
Typeset by KT Designs, St Helens
Printed in Poland

CONTENTS

ABBREVIATIONS

The following abbreviations are used in this book:

BR	British Rail
DEMU	Diesel Electric Multiple Unit
DMU	Diesel Multiple Unit
E&CHR	Easton & Church Hope Railway
GWR	Great Western Railway
LB&SCR	London, Brighton & South Coast Railway
L&SWR	London & South Western Railway
LMSR	London, Midland & Scottish Railway
MR	Midland Railway
S&D	Somerset & Dorset Railway
SR	Southern Railway
TUCC	Transport Users Consultative Committee
MVR	Moors Valley Railway
WS&WR	Wilts, Somerset & Weymouth Railway

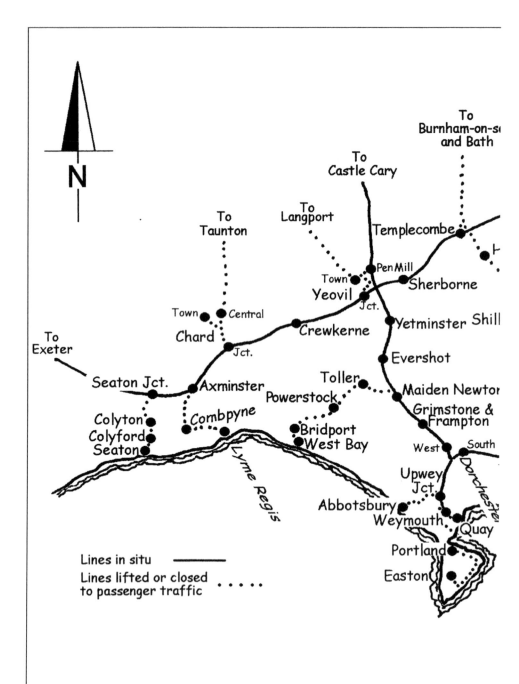

N

To Burnham-on-s⊢ and Bath

To Castle Cary

To Langport

To Taunton

Templecombe

Pen Mill

Town

Yeovil

Jct.

Sherborne

Town   Central

Chard

Jct.

Crewkerne

Yetminster Shill

To Exeter

Evershot

Seaton Jct.

Axminster

Toller

Powerstock

Maiden Newton

Colyton

Combpyne

Grimstone & Frampton

Colyford

Bridport

Seaton

West Bay

Lyme Regis

West   South

Dorchester

Upwey Jct.

Abbotsbury

Weymouth

Quay

Portland

Easton

Lines in situ ——————
Lines lifted or closed to passenger traffic • • • • •

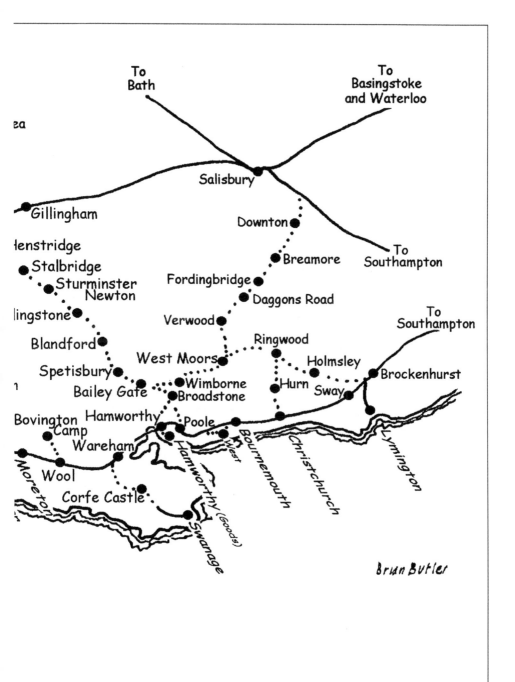

Brian Butler

Introduction

An old goods shed complete with loading gauge stands along a track off the B3157 not far from Abbotsbury village centre. Nearby can be found the remains of an engine shed where only the walls remain. A local resident claimed that the roof was removed a long time ago by the Great Western Railway (GWR) as an economy measure to save paying rates! The signal box has gone, also the water tower which was fed from a nearby stream. The station building was demolished some time ago to make way for a modern bungalow. Yet even here some of the past remains. The original platform edge can be determined and many of the stones from the station building have been used to construct a wall around the garden.

That same local resident, now in his 70s, recalled how as a boy he caught the 8.15 am train to Weymouth each day to attend school. He claimed, 'We walked miles to and from the station in those days. There aren't many kids like that any more.' The last train on the Abbotsbury Railway ran on 29th November 1952. More traffic was taking to the roads and so the railway failed, a situation all too typical of the many branch lines in Dorset that were to suffer a similar fate.

The first railway of a kind came to Dorset in October 1826. This was the Portland Railway, a primitive 4 ft 6 ins gauge line which ran from 400 ft above sea level down an inclined plane carrying stone from quarries to the sea for shipment. It was cable-worked with loaded wagons descending by gravity, hauling empty wagons up again in the opposite direction. Known as the 'Merchant's Railway' it continued to work until September 1939.

When conventional railways began to appear in the 1830s, Dorset was at first neglected. With a low population and very little heavy industry, the railway promoters were looking elsewhere for their profits. Yet in 1836 came a proposal, supported by the GWR, for a line from near Bath to run via

Dorchester to Weymouth. Unfortunately for the people of Dorset the Bill failed and was withdrawn from Parliament. The GWR was itself in its early days and was looking ahead too quickly.

Further proposals followed. One was from the South Western Railway to build a line from near Basingstoke to join the Bristol & Exeter Railway near Taunton, intending to serve the Dorset towns of Gillingham and Stalbridge. Another idea came from the London, Salisbury, Exeter & Falmouth Railway which proposed a line north of the county boundary but which would include a branch to Sherborne. Like the GWR proposal, these Bills were also withdrawn.

By the 1840s railways were booming and many plans were submitted. However, much of the time in Dorset was taken up with long and complicated battles between 'coastal' and 'central' parties and the need to decide on a trunk route towards Exeter. A local solicitor from Wimborne, Charles Castleman, played a great part in this when his independent company, the South-ampton & Dorchester, built a line to cross sparsely populated areas along a 'coastal' route. Castleman was confident that the London and South Western Railway (L&SWR) would continue on from Dorchester to Exeter but this did not happen. It was the 'central' party that eventually succeeded when the L&SWR built a line to Exeter from Salisbury.

A further complication at the time was a conflict over gauges. The GWR had chosen a broad gauge of 7 ft 0¼ ins whereas the L&SWR operated a narrow gauge system of 4 ft 8½ ins (later accepted as standard gauge). Despite early track problems and a 'Regulation of Gauge Act' introduced in 1846, the GWR retained its broad gauge for many years. Where different gauges met, such as at Dorchester, interchange of goods traffic became necessary. As time passed the narrow gauge gained popularity and in some cases 'mixed' gauge tracks, i.e. three rails, were laid. Where possible the GWR kept its broad gauge, considering this a protection against narrow gauge trains invading its territory.

The ensuing chapters cover the many branch lines that came into being, the majority of which later suffered under the Beeching axe. The Swanage Railway is included, being a prominent part — past and present — of Dorset's railway history. In addition, the opportunity is taken to look at those lines which crossed the county's border since these also played an important role.

This book sets out to examine the formation and lives of Dorset's railways as well as, where relevant, their decline and closure. It also provides the reader with a means to explore the many 'lost' stations that can still be found and trackbeds that have survived, some now converted to roads but others turned into footpaths.

Leslie Oppitz

Acknowledgements

Acknowledgements are due to the many libraries and record offices throughout Dorset where staff have delved into records, and to the following for their help in supplying many early pictures: John H. Meredith, Rod K. Blencowe, Stations UK and the late John Smith of Lens of Sutton. Thanks also to Bill Trite, Chairman of the Swanage Railway Company Ltd, for his considerable help and also for identifying many early locomotives.

Thanks also go to the following who assisted: the Proprietors of the Avon Causeway Hotel, Hurn; David Fletcher of the Bovington Tank Museum; Brian and Diana Read of the former Powerstock station; Jim Haylock of the Moors Valley Railway; The Royal Naval Base HMS *Osprey* on the Isle of Portland.

Personal thanks go to Brian Butler for his help in preparing the maps and to my wife, Joan, and daughter, Jackie, who toured Dorset with me. Thanks also go to my wife for her help in preparing and checking the manuscript and finally to the late Symi, our collie-cross dog, who took his first railway journey on the Swanage Railway.

1
A Route To The West

Salisbury/Templecombe/Yeovil/Exeter

Gillingham station opened 2nd May 1859 to become part of the L&SWR's main route to the South West. In this c1910 picture a Yeovil bound train awaits departure. (R.K.Blencowe)

Proposals to cross the county first came in the 1830s but it was not until some 20 years later that a decision was finally made on which route to the west should be taken. The action was to set much of the pattern for Dorset's railways of the future.

First ideas came when the GWR proposed a branch to link its line near Bath with Weymouth via Cerne Abbas and Dorchester. An extension to Weymouth Harbour was also envisaged which

An express passes through Sherborne station between Templecombe and Yeovil. When trains first reached Sherborne in May 1860 a general holiday was declared and church bells rang all day. (M.Wyatt/R.K.Blencowe)

could have led to a considerable enlargement of the harbour area. The plan came at a time when the GWR was hardly established and the Bill was withdrawn from Parliament.

Further ideas soon followed. A company, known as the South Western Railway, planned to leave the London & Southampton line at Basingstoke to join the Bristol & Exeter Railway at Taunton, to include intermediate stations at the Dorset towns of Gillingham and Stalbridge. Another, the London, Salisbury, Exeter & Falmouth Railway, planned to skirt the northern county border yet provided for a branch to Sherborne. Still another, the Durston & Salisbury Railway, proposed a route from Durston, near Taunton, to Salisbury again serving Sherborne by a branch line.

All these ideas failed for various reasons and it was not until 1844 that the 'battles' to establish routes across Dorset really began. Not only were rival companies involved but there was another problem. The GWR engineer, Isambard Kingdom Brunel, chose to build lines to a 'broad gauge' of 7 ft 0¼ ins whereas the London & South Western Railway (L&SWR) used a gauge of 4 ft 8½ ins (today's standard gauge).

Over the ensuing years further plans were submitted and withdrawn. It was not until 1847 that Parliament gave approval for an L&SWR-backed route from Salisbury to Yeovil. Agreement to build on from Yeovil to Exeter followed in July 1856. Alternative ideas submitted by the GWR were dropped and in the quest to reach Exeter, the rail gateway to Devon and Cornwall, the L&SWR narrow gauge had triumphed.

There was great excitement when the Salisbury & Yeovil Railway opened its first stretch from Salisbury to Gillingham on 2nd May 1859. The town was decorated and free beef, bread and beer was given to the sick. Beyond Gillingham there were problems when water from greensand caused trouble in the 742

Platforms 2 and 3 at Yeovil Junction photographed in 1959. When trains finally reached Exeter in July 1860 a special comprising 20 carriages hauled by 3 locomotives carried L&SWR directors and colleagues. (Stations UK)

13

yard Buckhorn Weston tunnel. Additional shafts had to be sunk to improve drainage. When trains reached Sherborne just over a year later on 7th May 1860, the day was declared a general holiday. Cannons were fired and church bells were rung. On 1st June 1860 trains reached Yeovil, terminating initially at the Bristol & Exeter line's station at Hendford.

Between Yeovil Junction and Exeter, some 3,000 men and 600 horses plus two locomotives were required to work on the 150 arches and bridges and 3,000,000 cubic yards of earthworks. At the 1,345 yard tunnel at Honiton water seepage problems had to be overcome. Finally on 18th July 1860 the long days of waiting were over. A special train of 20 carriages carrying L&SWR directors and Salisbury & Yeovil colleagues, hauled by *Britannia, Montrose* and *Vulcan*, reached Exeter Queen Street station (later Exeter Central).

The special train had left Waterloo at 8 am that morning but

Sutton Bingham station, 1964, between Yeovil and Crewkerne after closure in 1962. The station building has since been demolished. (Stations UK)

Crewkerne station looking westwards in 1964. The station's early buildings remain in use today although the track has been singled and the down platform no longer functions. (Stations UK)

beyond Yeovil it had stopped at each decorated station where speeches had been made by local dignitaries, often in heavy rain. At Exeter the occasion was marked, by coincidence of course, by a total eclipse of the sun! Some shops were shut and flags were displayed yet, according to the *Western Times,* the welcome was somewhat unenthusiastic. This was hardly surprising since trains on the GWR-backed Bristol & Exeter Railway had already reached the city via Taunton in triumph 16 years earlier.

Public services from Exeter began on 19th July 1860 with three trains each way daily. Two were to Waterloo and the other was to Yeovil. Full services began on 1st August 1860 when the L&SWR's first timetables were published for 1d monthly. The route of 171¼ miles could be covered in just over five hours with the speed averaging 33.2 mph including stops over the mostly single line route (doubling between Salisbury and Exeter was completed by 1867). In 1862 the L&SWR took the Salisbury &

15

The main platforms at Chard Junction station, c1930. Initially a short branch reached Chard Town station but when a Bristol & Exeter line reached the town from the north the lines were linked. (Stations UK)

Yeovil Railway on a 999-year lease which resulted in more effective control of the whole stretch. After many years of resistance to offers of outright purchase, the Salisbury & Yeovil finally gave way in 1878, yet selling to the L&SWR at a good price.

Subsequently much of the line from Exeter to Waterloo was well suited to high speeds and there was considerable competition against the GWR route to Paddington. Today a non-stop train from Exeter can reach Paddington in exactly two hours. By contrast today's trains on the 'L&SWR route' via Salisbury, where much of the route had been singled, take well over three hours with many stops. How that would have delighted GWR chiefs!

From 9th April 1904, a weekly London-bound high-speed L&SWR train was run to a schedule 20 minutes quicker than the GWR's best. Yet the rivalry was to bring disaster. On 30th June

1906 a five-coach special with 43 passengers waited at Templecombe while the engines were changed. A 4-4-0 locomotive no 421 backed on for the run non-stop to Waterloo and by the time the train reached Wilton it was travelling at 70 mph. It is still not known to this day why the driver, a man of considerable experience and a teetotaller, entered the 10 chain left-hand curve just beyond Salisbury station, a curve with a rigid 30 mph limit, with his whistle shrieking at such a high speed.

The train crashed and the coaches were reduced to matchwood. Locomotive no 421 left the track and ploughed through the vans of a train of empty milk churns in a nearby bay. More than half the passengers plus the driver and fireman were killed. Subsequently stricter speed limits were introduced and all passenger trains stopped at the station. Only the *Devon Belle* passed through Salisbury for a time to save congestion.

Templecombe's L&SWR station showing the Somerset & Dorset Joint Railway's platform where trains connected from Bath or Bridgwater. On the left the main-line through platforms. (R.K.Blencowe)

When Templecombe station between Gillingham and Sherborne closed on 7th March 1966 many thought it was lost forever, like so many other stations at that time, but in this instance life remained. Over the years since closure the local villagers campaigned to prove that, for Templecombe at least, Dr Beeching got it wrong. At one time it was an important junction where lines crossed as well as being joined by a loop and travellers changed trains to link with the Somerset & Dorset service. But the Somerset & Dorset also closed in 1966 and much of the station's importance was lost.

But the local folk were not deterred. Councillors and business-men set up action groups to get the station reopened. Persistent protests and arguments with British Rail eventually produced a result. BR said that if the station could be made usable at no cost to itself it would 'stop the odd train'. There was an immediate response. Local craftsmen volunteered services, villagers offered labour, pensioners dug trenches and help came too from lads at the nearby Borstal. The County Council contributed towards the overall cost.

The grand reopening came on 3rd October 1983. Celebrations rivalled those of May 1860 when the station first opened. Crowds arrived to see the first train symbolically break a banner stretched across the track. A special luncheon for council and railway dignitaries was held at the surviving railway hostelry, the Royal Hotel. It is a mark of achievement that today over 20 trains stop daily at Templecombe.

2
'Castleman's Corkscrew'

Southampton/Brockenhurst/Ringwood/
Broadstone/Hamworthy/Wareham

A Wimborne bound passenger train hauled by locomotive 30107 awaits departure from Bournemouth West in 1952. (R.K.Blencowe)

On 21st July 1845 the Southampton & Dorchester Railway obtained Parliamentary approval to build a line from South-ampton Central (then known as Blechynden) to Dorchester via Brockenhurst, Ringwood, West Moors, Wimborne and Ware-ham, plus a short branch to Poole (which later became known as Hamworthy Goods). The company had been formed in 1844 by a Wimborne solicitor, Charles Castleman, following a public

A mixed freight train passes through Wimborne station, c1930. At one time Somerset & Dorset trains reversed at Wimborne to reach Poole and Bournemouth. (Stations UK)

meeting held in May 1844 in Southampton. Castleman had been adamant from the start that the line could never survive on local traffic and he saw it only as a link in a trunk route to the west. Events have subsequently proved that it never took its place as a major cross-country route.

The proposed line was surveyed by Captain W.S. Moorsom, an experienced railway engineer. The route chosen was intended to give maximum benefit to a rather sparse area so its path through the various low hills and estuaries west of Southampton became a tortuous one. Because of this the line acquired the nickname of 'Castleman's Corkscrew' or 'the Water Snake'.

Much of the route was across open heathland so opposition from landowners to the new railway proved minimal. Good progress was made and by May 1847 the line was ready. Public opening was due on 1st June 1847 and many festivities were organised. However, two days before the event there was a disaster when part of a tunnel along the route at Southampton collapsed.

Support to the tunnel arch was necessary and this was carried out with timbers — which meant that through passage was now not possible! The only way to get the required rolling stock to the western end of the tunnel was by road and when the opening date came some trains did run on the official day. Despite the setback, celebrations at Ringwood went ahead with shops closing early and there was dancing on the green. Other festivities along the route were cancelled and a special dinner due to be held at the Crown Inn, Ringwood, took place a week later on 8th June 1847. Full services eventually started on 6th August.

The route can best be described by following the line from

Broadstone looking southwards, a junction for L&SWR trains to Brocken-hurst or Salisbury, also Somerset & Dorset trains to Templecombe and beyond. Broadstone has had numerous name changes including Poole Junction and Broadstone Junction. It became just Broadstone in 1956.(R.K.Blencowe)

West Moors station on the line from Brockenhurst to Broadstone, also a junction for trains to Salisbury via Fordingbridge. The station closed to passenger traffic in May 1964. (R.K.Blencowe)

Southampton. Starting from Northam junction, the railway turned in a westerly direction. After negotiating the tunnel, the track almost immediately reached what is now Southampton Central station (previously Blechynden). The westward direction continued as far as Redbridge before curving south to reach Brockenhurst. Beyond, the line crossed open country to reach Holmsley (Christchurch Road until 1863), Ringwood, West Moors (opened later in August 1867), Wimborne, Broadstone (opened as New Poole Junction) and beyond.

When the Southampton & Dorchester line opened, Bournemouth was a mere coastguard hamlet of about 30 houses whereas neighbouring Poole had a population of over 6,000. Although a busy port, it had been initially thought that Poole could not justify a branch. However, the town was enjoying a booming pottery trade and it was expected that the 60,000 tons of clay raised annually would compensate for any loss in

Wimborne station in June 1971, seven years after closure of the line to passenger traffic. The site later became Wimborne Industrial Estate. (R.K.Blencowe)

passenger traffic. As it transpired, neighbouring Bournemouth was soon to attract many visitors, and passengers to the town were using the Poole branch on a roundabout route to reach the new resort.

Initially there were five trains each way daily from South-ampton to Dorchester and these soon proved popular. A regular cattle market at Ringwood also guaranteed considerable addi-tional revenue. In 1848, a year after opening, the line was taken over by the L&SWR and Charles Castleman was given a seat on the board. In due course traffic increased sufficiently to a figure stipulated in the Act that allowed double track to be built. Work on this began in 1857 with completion on the whole section some six years later.

In 1862 a branch was opened from Ringwood to Christchurch via Hurn (chapter 3) which meant that Bournemouth passengers could now avoid the longer rail route via Poole. This new

Verwood on the Salisbury-West Moors line seen here in the 1950s. The station closed with the line in 1964, having lasted almost 100 years. (R.K.Blencowe)

development effectively made a backwater of the Ringwood section and brought about a reduction in traffic between Ringwood and Poole.

On 30th September 1935 the Ringwood to Christchurch branch closed completely. The Brockenhurst/Ringwood/West Moors line remained useful mainly for diversions and certain stopping passenger trains. In addition, through goods services between Southampton and Weymouth could take the line through Ringwood and so avoid congestion at Bournemouth.

Following the Beeching Plan of March 1963, the end was inevitable. A Transport Users Consultative Committee (TUCC) enquiry was held in Bournemouth both for the Ringwood line and the Salisbury/West Moors line also scheduled for closure, but there was little public opposition. The end for both lines came on 4th May 1964. On the Ringwood route, passenger services were withdrawn and the section between Brockenhurst and Ringwood closed completely. Ringwood continued to see

The Railway Hotel at Ringwood is all that remains to remind passers-by that a station once existed in the area, today lost to industrial development. (Author)

freight workings from the Wimborne end of the line for some years but these too were later suspended.

In contrast the section between Southampton and Brockenhurst was not only retained but it prospered. A line between Brockenhurst and Bournemouth had opened in 1888 with electrification to Bournemouth following some 80 years later in July 1967. In May 1988 electrification was completed to Weymouth. Today fast electric trains pass through Brockenhurst where once steam trains turned westwards to Ringwood. The curved path that remains is almost the only tangible reminder of the past.

After closure the remains of the Ringwood line were slowly removed piece by piece. First the track and sleepers were lifted, then anything else of possible scrap value was recovered. The next stage involved selling off the trackbed after which the new owners promptly erected fences across the former line. The station buildings came next. After a period of neglect those at

Following the demolition of Ringwood station, a newly-built road was named Castleman Way after Charles Castleman, a Wimborne solicitor, who formed the railway company in 1844. (Author)

Ringwood were demolished. Today the site is part of an industrial estate and the road built along the station trackbed is called, of course, 'Castleman Way'. Wimborne station is also difficult to locate. After massive earthworks to bring the whole area down to the adjacent road level, modern industrial units were constructed. Where once stood the station buildings, one can now haggle over the price of double glazing or possibly wall-to-wall carpeting.

Elsewhere, road improvements have cut across parts of the trackbed, yet long sections remain as footpaths. The Burley to Lymington road (close to the A35) passes where a platform still exists at the site of Holmsley station. The station building became a tea room where visitors could enjoy a meal or snack in what was once the station's waiting room. It could be easy to recall the

26

'Pioneer' leaves platform 2, Kingsmere station on the narrow gauge Moors Valley Railway located in the Moors Valley Country Park near Ringwood. (Photograph courtesy of Jim Haylock)

past in such surroundings. But it's no good expecting a train to come along. The last one left many years ago!

All that is left of West Moors station is the crossing keeper's cottage in Station Road. Yet if the noise of a railway engine whistle can be heard today while one is walking the old railway track between West Moors and Ringwood it will be from the nearby Moors Valley Country Park to be found off the Horton Road at Ashley Heath, just inside the Dorset border.

The 7¼ ins gauge Moors Valley Railway (MVR) could never be described as a mere entertainment for children. It is a highly competent railway system incorporating a mile of track which makes its way through cuttings and tunnels backed by an efficient signalling and points system controlled by a signal box with as many as 28 levers. The box opened in September 1988

27

with its levers previously in service at the premises of the Gas, Light & Coke Co of Beckton, East London.

Rolling stock includes some 15 steam locomotives with names such as *Sapper*, *Jason* and *Pioneer* and also includes numerous wagons and coaches. When the traffic is at its peak up to five trains can run at the same time. The maximum load hauled on the MVR so far comprised 16 coaches and 104 passengers.

The MVR started its life at Tuckton, near Bournemouth, but in 1986 it moved to its present more spacious site. The station, brick-built and covered, has three platforms and is styled architecturally from stations of the past. It is called Kingsmere, named after Kings Farm which previously occupied the area, with the station standing where there was once a cowshed!

3
An Early Line To Christchurch

Ringwood/Hurn/Christchurch

Ex-Southern Railway West Country class 4-6-2 no 34006 'Bude' hauling a Hampshire Explorer Special stops at Ringwood station on 21st May, 1966. (R.K.Blencowe)

With the Southampton & Dorchester Railway completed in 1847, access to Bournemouth for rail passengers meant travelling to Poole and then taking a rickety horse bus to complete the journey. For the inhabitants of Christchurch it was much the same. The nearest railway station was at Holmsley (opened as Christchurch Road) which required an eight mile journey by horse-drawn coach over windswept heathland.

In the 7th September 1935 edition of the *Christchurch Times,* an elderly resident reminisced over a journey to London in the late 1850s. A pony and trap had to leave Christchurch before daylight in order to catch a train at 9 am. Holmsley to London took five hours in railway coaches 'that were not built for comfort'. The local resident recalled, 'Ventilation was arrived at by a very crude method. One had to have the window either open or closed. The combustion of the fuel for the engine was likewise crude, with the result that our faces and clothes were pitted with black coal smuts.'

During Bournemouth's early days as a seaside resort, many of the local elite had fought hard to preserve its isolation. One local person claimed horror at 'the encroachments of the railway' and declared that 'it was bound to ruin the neighbourhood by taking from it all personality'. Yet as the trains came closer so the town's

Hurn station in L&SWR days c 1930, the only intermediate station between Ringwood and Christchurch. The station, initially called Herne Bridge, closed in September 1935. (Stations UK)

popularity increased. It was therefore inevitable that a more direct approach by rail should be considered. Eventually a group of railway promoters formed the Ringwood, Christchurch & Bournemouth Company and in 1859 powers were given to build a 7¾ mile line along the river Avon from Ringwood to Christchurch.

The line, worked by the L&SWR, opened on 13th November 1862 with Christchurch becoming the railhead for Bournemouth. The route chosen was from a junction west of Ringwood, turning south through the New Forest and across land owned by Lord Egmont. Fortunately he was a keen supporter of the new railway and made no objection to the route crossing his land. All he requested in return was a private station at which trains would stop at his request. This was granted and a halt was constructed taking the name Avon Lodge. The line had one other stopping place at Hurn where, in time for the opening in November 1862, a station complete with all the usual facilities had been established. Initially this was known as Herne Bridge; it was renamed Herne in 1888 and became Hurn in 1897 which it remained until closure.

The contractors for the line had been Messrs Brassey & Ogling. Funds had been short and in order to keep costs down the track had been constructed across heathland and through pine forests, avoiding any earthworks that were considered unnecessary. Consequently, with so many severe gradients and curves, trains were restricted to a speed limit of 25 mph. For a line that was to carry trains from London and Southampton to the fast-growing resort of Bournemouth, the promoters had shown very little ambition.

Initially three trains daily passed slowly each way between Ringwood and Christchurch. The journey time from London to Christchurch was now about four hours after which Bourne-mouth passengers faced an uncomfortable ride along rutted roads to the resort. The need for a rail extension became paramount and in 1863 an Act was obtained for the 3½ mile extension. However, progress was slow and the line was not completed until 14th March 1870 (chapter 4). Free rides were

The former Hurn station is today The Avon Causeway Hotel where many items of memorabilia can be found recalling the earlier days. A Pullman coach named the 'Avon Express' stands outside, providing additional seating for the hotel's customers. (Author)

given on the opening day to Bournemouth's new station which was later to become Bournemouth East station. It was a quarter of a mile east of the subsequent Central station and in due course the site of Bournemouth East station became part of the town's expanding goods depot.

The line from Ringwood to Bournemouth played no small part in the development of the resort. Through carriages from London were provided on Weymouth trains and these were detached or attached at Ringwood. On 1st January 1874, the Ringwood branch was formally absorbed by the L&SWR. In the same year, another branch reached Bournemouth from the west to terminate at the appropriately named Bournemouth West station.

As traffic to Christchurch and Bournemouth increased, the inconvenience of travelling on the time-consuming route via

At the entrance to the former Hurn station the original level crossing gate can still be found. (Author)

Ringwood became more apparent. In 1888 a direct route from Brockenhurst via Sway was opened to a junction at Christchurch where a new station was built. The original Christchurch station became part of the goods yard and the small engine shed was closed since the station was no longer a terminus and there was no need for such facilities.

It was soon apparent that the direct route via Sway would take all the traffic yet surprisingly the Ringwood/Christchurch branch remained in use for many years. Eventually on the evening of 28th September 1935, the last train to use the line left Bournemouth for Ringwood. The *Christchurch Times* reported, 'When services cease, Hurn station will close finally for all time. Its lights on the platform and in the signals will be extinguished and unbroken silence will descend upon the one-man station. The eight miles of track between Christchurch and Ringwood will be left to grass and rust. Maybe when the summer comes again the railway company will employ this length of rail to house some of their holiday homes, converted carriages let on hire to holiday-makers as summer bungalows.'

It seemed the greatest loss was to Mr H. Delia who had been acting station-master, chief clerk, ticket collector and porter at Hurn for the final eight years. He had no desire to leave Hurn where, reported the newspaper, he had 'lived happily in a cottage, if lonely at times. However, he has a dog for company'.

Today much of the route has become forest paths, while road schemes and buildings have cut across in places. The original Christchurch station has been totally obliterated by a modern industrial estate. Yet of what was a very short and obscure line, a few poignant reminders remain.

At Hurn station the former buildings have been converted into the Avon Causeway Hotel with an original level crossing gate still in existence. Inside the hotel many fascinating items of railway memorabilia can be found. A C1 coach named the *Avon Express* alongside the former platform provides additional seating for meals. Although popular with visitors, the coach is perhaps not quite what Mr Delia, the acting station-master of 1935, imagined for the future.

4
Lines Reach Bournemouth

Christchurch/Bournemouth/Poole

Poole station in the 1950s. A class M7 0-4-4T locomotive no 30028 with passenger set, probably an 'Old Road' service between Bournemouth West and Brockenhurst via Wimborne and Ringwood. (R.K.Blencowe)

Despite its size and popularity today, Bournemouth was very late to develop as a resort. Indeed, had not one day in 1810 a certain Captain Tregonwell and his rich wife chosen to drive along a rough moorland track from Mudeford, the town may not have grown as it did. Captain Tregonwell was delighted with the area as he came upon it and decided at once to buy land and build a house. It was not long before he had planted the valley

35

and much of the coast with many of the pines that subsequently made the town famous. The house that he built himself was on the site of what is now the Royal Exeter Hotel near The Square.

When powers were granted for a line to be built from Ringwood to Christchurch in 1859, Bournemouth came closer to a line reaching it from the east. Services began in November 1862 and visitors to Bournemouth had the option of reaching the resort from either Poole or Christchurch although in each case a horse-drawn bus was needed. In 1863 an Act was agreed for a line from Christchurch to Bournemouth although the work was not completed until 14th March 1870. Many Bournemouth residents were apprehensive about the prospect of trains bringing 'trippers' and the like into their town and because of this the station was built on the very outskirts. The buildings were small and quite inadequate, being little better than huts, yet as time passed the residents began to complain about the condition of their station! In addition, residents in the fast-

Christchurch station photographed in 1965. On either side of the station three-span bowstring bridges cross the Avon and Stour rivers. (Stations UK)

growing areas of Pokesdown and Boscombe began asking for local stations but the L&SWR refused.

Meantime in September 1863 a line had opened threatening the L&SWR routes. The Somerset & Dorset Railway (S&D) completed a through route from Highbridge on the Bristol Channel through Templecombe to Wimborne where trains reversed to complete the journey to Poole over L&SWR metals. Subsequently in December 1866 the Salisbury & Dorset Junction Railway opened a line from Salisbury to West Moors on the Southampton & Dorchester line. The L&SWR, seeing a threat to its monopoly, decided to work the line to West Moors from the outset which meant that Salisbury now had a direct route to the coast at Poole. Poole station was situated some distance from Poole town centre so visitors going on to Bournemouth had not only to walk across the Harbour bridge (paying a toll) but also take the horse bus from Poole town centre for the remainder of their journey. The remoteness of the original Poole station (now

A passenger train headed by LMS 696 at Parkstone station, between Bournemouth and Poole, c1930. Beyond the station, the line skirts Parkstone Bay, with fine views of Brownsea Island and the Isle of Purbeck. (Stations UK)

37

Locomotive 53806 at Branksome in the 1950s. A siding at Branksome gives access to a Motive Power Depot. Branksome station dates from 1874 with the opening of the line from Poole to Bournemouth West. (R.K.Blencowe)

known as Hamworthy Goods) from the town remained a problem until 2nd December 1872 when a section of track from Broadstone was completed to a new station in the town centre. The location was also chosen since it left the promoters in a more favourable position to extend towards Bournemouth. As trains began to use the new Poole station, the original Poole station was renamed Hamworthy. Traffic on the original branch dwindled and Hamworthy closed to passenger traffic in 1896 to become Hamworthy Goods.

The Broadstone to Poole line had been started by the independent Poole & Bournemouth Railway but in July 1871 the L&SWR successfully obtained powers to take it over. On 15th June 1874 a ¾ mile line to serve Poole Quay was opened. Trains ran through the streets around the west side of the town and along the quay to reach what was known as the 'fishing shambles'. Two B4 0-4-OT locomotives worked the short branch. Just over a month later an extension from the new Poole station to the western end of Bournemouth was completed and, unlike the station on the line from Christchurch, the West station was well constructed and generally approved of by the local people.

Bournemouth West station opened on 15th June 1874. There were some eight trains in and out daily, these being initially S&D services joining L&SWR metals at Wimborne. For the S&D, reaching Bournemouth had been a triumph indeed. Within a short time, a through route from Bournemouth to Bristol, the Midlands and the North of England could be offered although, disappointingly for the promoters, the line never achieved the success it might have expected.

Meantime, with Bournemouth's population continuing to expand, dissatisfaction continued over the inadequacy of the East station. Pressure also continued from the residents of Pokesdown and Boscombe for local stations but the L&SWR still refused. However, in 1882 the L&SWR received approval to build a cut-off line from Brockenhurst to Christchurch through the New Forest via Sway. This meant that the distance from Waterloo to Bournemouth would become $8\frac{1}{2}$ miles shorter and also that the time-consuming Ringwood-Christchurch route could be avoided.

Construction of the cut-off began the following year. Serious difficulties due to earth slippage were encountered during the building of an embankment at Sway. Even though the height was only 60 ft, it was necessary for the base to be 500 ft wide. On 20th July 1885 Bournemouth got a new 'East' station built to the west of the original. Designed by William Jacomb, the L&SWR's Chief Engineer, the station had a covered roof 350 ft long and 100 ft wide. Despite its improvement on the previous station, there were many local residents who were not happy and who expressed pleasure that it was 'hidden' in a cutting!

Also during 1885 a further attempt was made to break the L&SWR's monopoly at Bournemouth. The Didcot, Newbury & Southampton Railway, backed by the GWR, unsuccessfully attempted a line from Whitchurch. Perhaps it was no coincidence that during the following year the inhabitants of Pokesdown and Boscombe got their local stations. Finally on 14th December 1885 a 2¾ mile cut-off was completed from Corfe Mullen junction to Broadstone so that S&D trains no longer had to reverse at Wimborne but could travel directly through to Bournemouth West.

The 'Sway line' cut-off from Brockenhurst to Christchurch was ready for use on 5th March 1888. The new route meant that faster speeds would be possible and there could be an increase of traffic capacity. The splitting of the Bournemouth and Weymouth portions from Waterloo was transferred from Ringwood to Brockenhurst. To celebrate the opening, a William Adams locomotive 4-4-0, no 526, hauled eleven coaches including the Director's Saloon the entire 107½ miles from Waterloo to

Hamworthy station c1930. Hamworthy was first known as Poole station serving Poole and Bournemouth. It became Hamworthy in 1872 when a section of track from Broadstone was completed to a new Poole station in the town centre. When Hamworthy closed to passengers in 1896 it became known as Hamworthy Goods. (Stations UK)

40

Bournemouth making numerous stops on the way. On the same day a connecting link was opened between Bournemouth's East and West stations.

The popularity of Bournemouth as a resort was greatly enhanced by its excellent train services from many directions. In 1900 the comfort of passengers was improved when a Pullman car was put in service. Pullmans had been tried before on the L&SWR as early as 1880 on the Exeter route but they had not proved successful. The idea worked for a time on the Bournemouth trains but as corridor stock and dining cars were introduced, the Pullmans were gradually withdrawn lasting until around 1911.

During the 1890s there were further notable events. On 1st June 1893 a link was completed between Hamworthy Junction and Poole. The line, known as the Holes Bay curve, crossed

Hamworthy Junction, c1930, on the main Christchurch, Bournemouth and Dorchester line. Originally it was named Poole Junction, then it became Hamworthy Junction, finally it was renamed just Hamworthy in 1972. (Stations UK)

41

shallow tidal water and allowed Weymouth trains to pass through Bournemouth. Because of this the original main-line traffic that travelled via Wimborne and Ringwood declined since passengers were now able to take a more direct route. On the same day, an avoiding line was completed at Branksome which meant that it was no longer necessary to reverse trains at Bournemouth West.

Finally on 1st July 1896, the original Poole station (now Hamworthy Goods) closed to passengers. The branch remained open for freight and it has survived to this day. The passenger

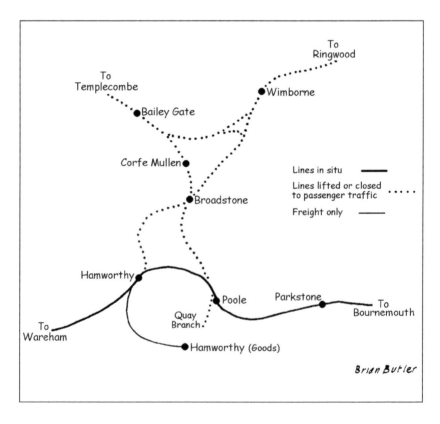

platform can still be found although the station buildings have long since gone. There were once stables alongside the station which accommodated horses used for shunting but these buildings have also gone. At one time the station overlooked Poole Harbour with the water often reaching the track edge but this stopped when Poole Yacht Club built on the adjacent 'reclaimed' land.

During the early part of the 20th century many through long-distance services reached Bournemouth via the S&D line. These included an all-the-year-round Manchester/Bournemouth restaurant car train which started on 1st October 1910 and later to be known as the *Pines Express*. In the early 1930s the Southern Railway, formed after 'grouping' in 1923, introduced Pullman cars to its lines. On 5th July 1931 the *Bournemouth Belle*, a new all-Pullman express, commenced services.

On 2nd May 1960 the ¾ mile Poole Quay line which ran through the streets closed. The S&D was struck a deathblow in September 1962 when the *Pines Express* was re-routed via Reading and Basingstoke. On 4th May 1964 the Wimborne/Ringwood/Brockenhurst line, redundant to through passenger trains since the Sway cut-off, fell victim to the Beeching axe. It was only a matter of time before the S&D followed. Bournemouth West closed on 6th September 1965 and the S&D closure followed about six months later on 7th March 1966.

It was to be expected that electrification to Bournemouth would follow. Some services commenced during 1966 but full services became available on 10th July 1967. Following the elimination of steam on the Southern Region, Bournemouth could be reached from Waterloo in 100 minutes. Previously Bournemouth station had four through tracks and two through platforms but with electrification this was reduced to two tracks only, one per platform, with the short bay platform used for stopping trains. The west end of the station included a short siding for the diesel locomotive which would wait to take on the Weymouth portion.

Electrification to Weymouth was completed in May 1988. New air-conditioned class 442 trains, capable of speeds of up to 100 mph, can today be seen along the route. They seem a far cry from those early steam trains which, in the middle of the 19th century, chugged their way across the New Forest to reach within about six miles of Bournemouth, a resort that at the time hadn't even come into being!

5
Westwards To Dorchester

Poole/Wareham/Bovington Camp/Dorchester

Wareham's first station was built in 1847 but when the Swanage branch opened in 1885 a new station was built on the present site. The first station, east of the level crossing, closed in 1887. In this picture, Wareham, c1930, plus one onlooker! (Stations UK)

Should you be visiting Moreton near Dorchester and you see someone wildly riding a motorcycle through the village lanes with Arab robes flowing behind him, then, according to local hearsay, it is the ghost of T.E. Lawrence, Lawrence of Arabia. It was a love of fast motorcycles that caused his untimely death in 1935 on a quiet Moreton road when speeding from his Clouds Hill home to the village post office. Yet he is still remembered today. His effigy has pride of place at Wareham church which

Holton Heath station, c1935, between Poole and Wareham opened with the line in 1847. The station served the Admiralty during the First World War when a narrow-gauge railway network was constructed from sidings to a cordite factory. (Stations UK)

Lawrence much loved. His reclining figure can be seen in Arab costume, his head resting on a camel.

Moreton is one of the intermediate stations between Hamworthy and Dorchester, the final stretch of line opened by the Southampton & Dorchester Railway (L&SWR from 1848) on 1st June 1847. Stations westwards from Broadstone included Hamworthy Junction (opened as Poole Junction), Holton Heath and Wareham (the Swanage branch followed in 1885) and then on towards Wool where a two mile long military branch line opened to Bovington Camp in 1919. Next came Moreton and finally the terminus at Dorchester (today known as Dorchester South).

Hamworthy's present station comprises two platforms, complete with canopies, linked by a subway with the small, red brick, main buildings on the up side. Westwards towards

46

Wareham station today, between Poole and Dorchester South. In the early 1920s, some 15 trains daily left for Swanage with three on Sundays. (Author)

Wareham a bridge carries the line over the entrance to Lychett Bay. Before Wareham comes Holton Heath, a station which was used by the Admiralty during the First World War to serve a depot on the up side where an extensive narrow gauge railway network was constructed from sidings to a cordite factory. The station became available for public use from 14th July 1924.

Wareham's first station was built in 1847. When the Swanage branch opened on 2nd May 1885 a new station, not completed until 1887, was constructed on the present site. The original station was situated to the east of the level crossing, the latter having long since gone following the building of the town's bypass. Opposite Wareham station today is the Railway Hotel where any rail enthusiast cannot fail but admire the picture of locomotive no 453, *King Arthur*, depicted in tiles on a wall facing the line. Between Wareham and Worgret junction the line crosses the river Piddle. There is a story that when Queen Victoria

47

visited the area by train she was told it was the river Trent so that her Royal dignity should not be offended!

At Worgret junction trains still leave the main line to reach Furzebrook sidings to serve an oil terminal and also one of the clay works for which the area was previously famous. One Train Working applies to the three mile branch and there is a maximum speed limit of 20 mph. This is part of the line that once led across the Purbeck Hills to Swanage.

Wool station lost its 1847 down side buildings in the early 1970s. Instead today there is a modern ticket office plus a mere shelter on the up side. Yet for many people Wool must surely bring to mind the writings of Thomas Hardy. The nearby Manor, the old seat of the Turbervilles, is popularly accepted as the place where Tess Durbeyfield spent her honeymoon night. To hundreds of servicemen Wool is perhaps better remembered by the nearby Bovington Camp, the home base for many

Wareham's station building, September 2000. The station with its Dutch gable carries the date of 1886. (Author)

On the wall of the Railway Hotel at Wareham can be found this likeness of 'King Arthur' locomotive 4-6-0 no 453. (Author)

tankmen. The Tank Museum which started its life in 1923 as the Royal Tank Corps Museum is today visited by large numbers of people. Armoured fighting vehicles from both World Wars stand proudly recalling the past and the author remembers more than one visit to remind him of his days (1944-1948) with the 4th Royal Tank Regiment!

In addition to tracks built to the nearby Lulworth army ranges, a branch line for military working only opened in 1919 from Wool station to Bovington Camp. Work on the line began in early 1918 and the first train conveying four tanks ran from the camp to Wool station around 16th February 1919. About 100 POWs were used to assist in construction and they were accommodated in huts either at Bovington or Wool. Initially the railway was operated by the War Department with regular deliveries of tanks being made but on 9th August 1919 the line was handed over to the L&SWR who provided passenger stock.

Wool station, 1965. In earlier times before motor cars took over from rail travel, Wool was well known to people visiting Lulworth Cove. (R.K.Blencowe)

Wool station today where the original 1847 down side buildings have been replaced by a modern ticket office and just a shelter on the up side. (Author)

After the First World War, many tanks were presented to towns all over Britain which had raised large sums in War Bond drives. The tanks were to be put on display — whether they were wanted or not. The line to Bovington Camp closed completely on 4th November 1928 although traces of the track can be found today between Wool and the camp. A recent acquisition at Bovington has been a railway wagon, originally acquired from British Rail in Wales, converted to an Armoured Train Truck. The vehicle carries a short ex-First World War six-pounder gun which is genuine and which was once used on an armoured train.

It is worth recording that a few years ago at Bovington there was an amusing, yet dignified, ceremony when a party of German officers arrived bearing two crates of champagne asking, 'Could we have one of our tanks back please?' The museum, which had two of the particular type, was able to oblige.

Wool station, seen here 1908, is remembered by servicemen who trained at the nearby Bovington Camp, a home base for many tank men. A branch to the camp opened in 1919. (Stations UK)

51

The branch from Wool to Bovington Camp closed in November 1928. As can be seen from the supports in this March 1951 picture, traces of the line remained for many years. (R.K.Blencowe)

A First World War Mk IV tank with its gun supports removed being taken by rail away from Bovington Camp after the Second World War probably to be presented as a 'memento' to a town which had raised large sums in War Bonds. (Picture courtesy of the Tank Museum, Bovington Camp)

Moreton, near Dorchester, where a visitor can be reminded of Thomas Hardy. It was to this little station that Tess Durbeyfield drove Angel Clare to watch milk churns being loaded into a London train. Today the 1847 station has gone – this picture was taken in 1959. (Stations UK)

Moreton station photographed in September 2000. Nearby is the Frampton Arms public house where many items of railway memorabilia can be found. (Author)

Dorchester South station, c1930. The former down platform terminus can be seen to the left. This was constructed with an extension to Exeter in mind although this never materialised. (Stations UK)

At Moreton, the last station before Dorchester, the visitor can be reminded of Thomas Hardy once again. It was to this little station that Tess Durbeyfield drove Angel Clare to watch milk churns being loaded into a London train. It was at Moreton she sheltered from the rain under a holly tree. The 1847 Moreton station building with its gabled up side has gone with only today's basic requirements remaining. To recall the past, visit the nearby Frampton Arms where a display of old railway pictures can be seen.

The end of the line came at Dorchester with the station built as a terminus yet planned with an extension to Exeter in mind. The latter of course never materialised although when the broad gauge GWR came ten years later, on 20th January 1857, passengers at Dorchester had additional access to Weymouth to the south and Yeovil and beyond to the north. To achieve this the L&SWR had to build a link line connecting to the GWR tracks with interchange of goods traffic carried out in the

54

Dorchester South station on the electrified Waterloo-Weymouth line. The former terminus to the right has been demolished. (Author)

L&SWR yard where mixed gauge rails met.

Dorchester became unique with its up platform a terminus and its down platform on the through line to Weymouth. All up trains from Weymouth therefore had to reverse in order to call at Dorchester. The platform arrangement lasted until 1970 when a new up platform was constructed on a 20 mph restricted curve plus a causeway for passengers connecting the new with the old over the original terminus trackbed.

On 25th November 1986 Dorchester South acquired a new main building and a redesigned forecourt as part of a multi-thousand pound redevelopment partnership between Eldridge Pope & Co plc, the Dorchester brewers, and British Rail, Southern Region. Eldridge Pope's 'sponsorship' agreement with BR made it the first such agreement between BR and a private sector company.

The well known Dorset firm of brewers began in 1833 when

This plaque at Dorchester South commemorates the joint venture between EP & Co (Eldridge Pope and Co, Brewers) and British Rail when the station was redesigned in 1986. (Author)

The former station-master's house at Dorchester South was opened as a public house in the summer of 1989. (Author)

Charles Eldridge and his wife Sarah took over the Antelope Hotel in Dorchester. Within four years its success led to the establishment of the Green Dragon Brewery. Charles Eldridge died in 1846, yet the brewery continued to expand and in 1880 the present brewery was built. Today over 120 years later Alfred Pope's grandson and three great grandsons continue to maintain the old traditions and the brewery owns nearly 200 pubs, some as far away as London and Bristol. The brewery, with considerable foresight, was built close to the railway giving easy access through to Poole, Bournemouth and Southampton and on to Winchester and Portsmouth. As a permanent reminder of the company's involvement with Dorcheser South, the station building carries a plaque reading 'E P & Co 1986'.

Dorchester South's old terminus buildings have been demolished and, in contrast, the nearby former station-master's house has been refurbished. It opened on 1st June 1989 as a public house called, of course, the Station Master's House with the Victorian style of architecture maintained throughout. When the pub was opened officially on 18th July 1989, the last station-master to live in the house, John Smith, was present at the ceremony.

When cartographer Emmanuel Bowen described Dorchester back in 1760, he observed, ' 'Tis also famous for brewing the best and finest beer in England'. There are surely many today who might well agree with him.

57

6

A Line From Wiltshire

Salisbury/Fordingbridge/West Moors

Fordingbridge station in the 1950s. Today there is virtually no sign of Fordingbridge station where the site became an industrial area. Only the name Station Road has survived the years. (R.K.Blencowe)

Despite its authorisation on 22nd July 1861, the Salisbury & Dorset Junction Railway took over five years to build. The line, intended to bring about a 'much-needed improvement between Salisbury and the Dorset coast', left the Salisbury to Bishopstoke branch at Alderbury junction to join the Southampton & Dorchester 'Corkscrew' branch at West Moors. The route had originally been planned to reach the coast with Poole included in

Daggons Road station with its single platform opened in 1856. A dead-end siding at the station was converted to a loop in 1904 to facilitate shunting. The station, seen here in the 1950s, closed in 1964 and the area is today private properties. (R.K.Blencowe)

the title but the Act covered only the line to West Moors.

Construction of the single track 19 mile railway commenced in February 1864, nearly three years after approval, and engineer to the project was Hamilton Henry Fulton. Unlike Fulton's previous project, the Stokes Bay branch in Hampshire, the Salisbury & Dorset involved many steep gradients and sharp curves and these caused delays. Later in 1864 there was a problem when work was delayed for three months due to the failure of a contractor. Afterwards work proceeded at a slow rate and opening eventually took place on 20th December 1866.

There were five intermediate stations. These were Verwood, Daggons Road, Fordingbridge, Breamore and Downton with the single track providing passing loops at each. There were also no less than six level crossings, while north of Fordingbridge there was a private siding serving a Government store. Each station

59

When visited by the author in September 2000, Breamore's 'Station House'
was occupied by 87-year-old 'Dinky' Trim, the wife of the late Leslie Trim who
had been in charge of the station. (Author)

had facilities for handling goods as well as passengers with
Fordingbridge by far the largest, having four sidings as well as
separate cattle pens and a goods warehouse.

Initially the independent line was worked by the L&SWR.
Only one of the intermediate stations, Verwood, was in Dorset.
West Moors, at the junction of the Southampton & Dorchester,
was opened the following year on 1st August 1867. A further
station, Alderholt, opened in March 1876 but the name was
changed to Daggens Road (later spelt Daggons Road). The line
offered a saving in time and distance against the earlier route
from Salisbury to Poole via Brockenhurst and Ringwood.

In 1878 the independent Bournemouth Direct Railway
proposed an extension from West Moors to Bournemouth which
would have given the Salisbury & Dorset Junction Railway direct
access to the resort. The L&SWR of course opposed the idea since
it would have threatened its own routes to Bournemouth and the

proposal never materialised. In August 1883 the L&SWR took over the Salisbury to West Moors line completely.

On 3rd June 1884 there was a disastrous accident when the 4.33 pm service from Salisbury was derailed between Downton and Breamore killing five passengers and injuring another 41. The train was reported to have been travelling at nearly 70 mph, well in excess of the speed allowed. The incident drew immediate attention to the poor state of the rolling stock and also the inadequate ballast along the track. This was a situation that had become typical of many backwater and non-profit-making branch lines. In its report, the Railway Inspectorate of the Board of Trade was highly critical over such failures. At Downton, the condition of the track had even been noticed by an outsider, the daughter of the local Rector, who found places where a number of keys had fallen out of the track chairs so the rails were no longer adequately secured.

In the early 1920s some six trains each way called at Breamore on weekdays travelling between Bournemouth West and Salisbury, most with London (Waterloo) connections. (R.K.Blencowe)

61

This is all that remains today of Breamore station building which closed to all traffic in 1964. (Author)

During its life the line settled for a quiet existence. From its earliest days it remained a backwater with the L&SWR deliberately keeping services meagre for fear it took traffic away from its own system. Yet the line proved useful to some extent as a diversion for north-south trains, in particular when the neighbouring Somerset & Dorset line was overburdened. Several peak Saturday services used the route, especially during the 1950s, although the journey usually took longer. Another notable through service that survived a number of years was the overnight newspaper train from Wateroo to Weymouth via Salisbury.

In March 1963 the 'Beeching Plan' was published. Notice of closure of the Salisbury-West Moors line was announced very soon afterwards, at the end of June 1963. It was one of the first in the country to follow the plan's publication. Rising operating costs and wages had taken their toll and it was clear that

Cars race past where once stood West Moors station. All that survives is the crossing keeper's cottage in Station Road. (Author)

stopping trains of three carriages with no more than 20 passengers could hardly pay their way. In fact closure had already been under consideration when the plan was published.

On 3rd March 1964 the Minister of Transport announced his consent to the closure subject to the provision of extra buses. This was to be effective from Monday, 4th May, with the last trains running on the previous Saturday. The same day also saw the end of passenger services from Brockenhurst to Broadstone via West Moors.

According to the *Salisbury Journal,* it was a night to remember when the last train left Salisbury bound for Bournemouth at 8.30 pm on that final Saturday. A wreath bearing the legend 'Last passenger train to Bournemouth' was ceremoniously placed on the front of the locomotive, the reigning Fordingbridge Carnival Queen, Miss Valerie Knibbs, kissed the engine-driver and Salisbury's station-master, Mr S.J. Cooney, blew the final whistle. On board the streamer-bedecked train there were hundreds of people anxious to claim the memory of the last ride.

Passengers included more than 70 members of the Fording-bridge Camera Club, armed to the teeth with equipment, who were determined to commit the occasion to film. Along the line, crowds waved their personal farewells and 'Down with Beeching' posters were to be seen. Fordingbridge station was floodlit for photographers but such were the crowds that taking pictures proved difficult. A reporter quoted an elderly man, sandwiched between a teenager and a stout lady trying to protect a stylish hat, as shouting, 'It's like VE Day all over again!'

For many the night did not end with the last journey. The Carnival Queen and her attendants, the members of the Camera Club and members of the station staff were invited to a wine and cheese supper at the Fighting Cocks at Godshill. At 3 pm the next afternoon there was a strange occurrence. Many folk in Fordingbridge claimed that they heard an engine's whistle and a familiar chugging noise. Yet nobody actually saw 'the train' and the authorities denied its existence. Possibly for some the celebrations of the previous evening had lasted longer than expected!

At Fordingbridge today there is hardly a trace of the station which was sited to the west of the town although Station Road and Station Garage remain in evidence. When the author visited Breamore in September 2000, the station building was still there although somewhat neglected over the 36 years since closure. 'Station House' was occupied by 87-year-old 'Dinky' Trim, the widow of the late Leslie Trim who was in charge of the station. On the small platform were signs where a signal box had stood and, after closure, a nearby goods building became for a time a depot for United Dairies although a later owner specialised in walnut furniture.

At Daggons Road, close to the village centre of Alderholt, the station has been completely demolished. The site is today occupied by a bungalow and two houses, appropriately called Railway Cottages. During the First World War, Alderholt had unexpected visitors when soldiers arrived by mistake instead of at their intended destination, Aldershot.

The Salisbury-West Moors line set out originally to become a valuable link between Salisbury and Bournemouth as well as provide a useful through route from Waterloo to Poole via Salisbury. Yet the track remained single throughout its life and never reached main-line status. It could truly be described as 'a line that might have been'.

7

The Somerset & Dorset Railway

Bournemouth to Evercreech Junction

Ex-LMS Fowler class 4F 0-6-0 no 44560 heads a Somerset & Dorset passenger train as it enters Broadstone station in 1951. (B.Knowlman/ R.K.Blencowe)

The 69¾ mile Somerset & Dorset (S&D) line that linked the Bristol Channel with the South Coast had many descriptions in its time. Perhaps those who suffered from some of its short-comings agreed with the 'Slow and Dirty' version whereas enthusiasts who enjoyed travelling the line with its superb scenery preferred 'Serene and Delightful'. The S&D was never

Ex-LMS class 2P 4-4-0 no 40697 heads a passenger train as it passes through Spetisbury Halt in July 1950. (S.C.Townroe/R.K.Blencowe)

prosperous and it could never have been described as efficient, but it certainly won the hearts of many.

Looking back to its early years, it seems strange that the S&D began not only with two separate railways, the Somerset Central and the Dorset Central, but also different gauges. The Somerset Central, although independent, had been formed in 1852 under the wing of the Bristol & Exeter and the Dorset Central came out of an abortive 1852 scheme for a South Midland Union Railway.

The first section (broad gauge) was opened to regular traffic on 28th August 1854 by the Somerset Central with a line from Highbridge Wharf to Glastonbury. Highbridge was favoured since the railway could use the route of the Glastonbury Canal which had previously been sold and closed. In addition Highbridge was considered a potential steamer port which could usefully handle passenger traffic to Wales. On 3rd May 1858 the Somerset Central opened an extension to Burnham-on-Sea (eventually to become the Bristol Channel outlet of the S&D)

67

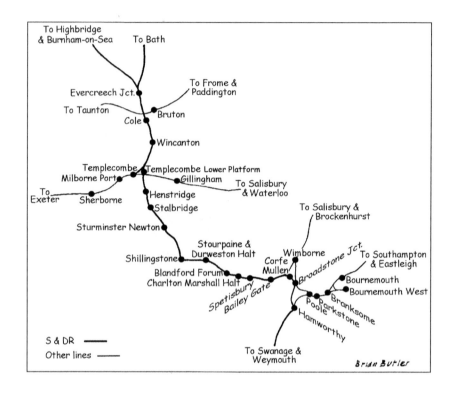

where trains could run onto a 900 ft pier. The following year, on 15th March 1859, a further line was opened from Glastonbury to Wells with the intention, at that time, of linking with the Wilts, Somerset & Weymouth Railway.

The next stretch of the S&D came from the Dorset Central which opened a (narrow gauge) line from Wimborne Junction to a temporary station at Blandford on 1st November 1860 to be initially worked by the L&SWR. Blandford was originally known as Blandford St Mary, then a small village to the south-west of the main town. There were intermediate stations at Charlton Marshall and Spetisbury. The first sod of the Dorset line had been cut at Blandford on 13th November 1856 by Lady Smith of Down House. The expenses for the ceremony came to well over

The 3.35 pm train from Bournemouth West to Bath headed by ex-LMS class 2P 4-4-0 no 40601 about to leave from Poole station in April 1949 on the Somerset & Dorset line. (R.K.Blencowe)

£200 including £71 for wine. This was a surprisingly large amount bearing in mind the company's uncertain future.

In the meantime the Somerset Central planned a route from Glastonbury to Cole near Bruton. This would eventually link with the Dorset line in anticipation of forming the much sought-after Channel-to-Channel link. In addition Somerset Central shareholders voted for conversion to narrow gauge since it was appreciated that with different gauges there would be no through route to the south. The Somerset Central sought Parliamentary approval to abandon broad gauge on its Cole extension. This did not prove easy and the Bill was modified to require mixed gauge to be built.

The line to Cole opened to public traffic on 3rd February 1862 and a section of Dorset Central line reaching Cole from Templecombe opened on the same day. Initially the Somerset Central worked the lines (narrow gauge) on either side of Cole

69

and provided the rolling stock. Throughout these events it became inevitable that the two companies would amalgamate to work as one and, following special meetings, a Bill for Amalgamation was submitted to Parliament. This was agreed on 7th August 1862 to take effect from 1st September 1862. The Somerset & Dorset Railway had come into being.

The final 16 miles between Templecombe and Blandford were completed by 31st August the following year and, with the L&SWR allowing S&D trains to reverse at Wimborne, trains could continue to Poole (now Hamworthy). For the first time a continuous rail route connected the two coasts. In 1865 the S&D chartered the SS *Albion* to provide a Poole-Cherbourg link claiming a through service from South Wales and the North. Goods traffic increased but it was not enough to stave off the troubles that were to come.

Following periods of 'railway mania', 1866 proved a year of financial crisis to many railway companies. The S&D found itself very short of funds with a need to borrow from the revenue account to pay for much of the narrow gauge stock and other equipment. Endeavours to raise fresh capital proved hopeless so a receiver was appointed. Although no property was seized, many locomotives ran only with the reluctant agreement of the creditors with some bearing owners' plates to show they were no longer S&D property. Many were surprised that the company had not tried to sell out but the S&D resolved to keep going. The company remained in receivership until 1870 by which time prospects improved somewhat and the court agreed that the company could raise further capital in debentures.

In 1872 the problem of the remoteness of the original Poole station had been solved when a section of track from Broadstone was completed to a new Poole station in the town centre. On 15th June 1874 Bournemouth West station opened. Through Somerset & Dorset trains were at last possible from Bournemouth to the Midlands and the North.

In June 1874 a line was built between Evercreech, north of Templecombe, and a Midland Railway (MR) line at Bath. The MR had just reached Bath and was interested in the prospect of a

Corfe Mullen Halt photographed in 1964 eight years after its closure. Corfe Mullen, together with other halts on the Somerset & Dorset line, closed in 1956 as an economy measure. (Stations UK)

narrow gauge link with Bournemouth giving access to and from the Midlands and the North. When the extension opened four trains daily were scheduled, two of these carrying through coaches from Birmingham. The first train which left Bath at 7.25 am was well and truly fêted along the route. Flags were flown and church bells rang out and crowds at Evercreech and Wincanton were such that the train was delayed and a connection with an Exeter train at Templecombe was missed. Interest in the new line was such that the Evercreech to Burnham line was now looked on as a branch.

When a connecting link between the S&D and the L&SWR opened in 1870 at Templecombe, a substantial amount of goods traffic between Bath and the L&SWR line resulted. However, despite such improvements, troubles persisted. The S&D had overstretched itself and, as well as general financial problems, locomotives and rolling stock were fast wearing out. The only solution appeared to be to find a buyer. The GWR and the Bristol & Exeter, when approached, suggested that the L&SWR might like to take the line south of Templecombe but the L&SWR when hearing of the GWR interest was determined to curtail any GWR involvement. Whilst appearing to be considering the offer made, the L&SWR had hurried consultations with the Midland Railway which had a through narrow gauge interest from Bath. The result was a joint offer agreed with the S&D, more favourable than that provisionally offered by the GWR and the Bristol & Exeter. Considerable bad feeling existed between the GWR and the L&SWR following these tactics and it was some time before the matter was forgotten

The Somerset & Dorset Joint Railway came into being by an Act of 13th July 1876 which agreed a take-over by the L&SWR and the MR on equal terms through a 999-year lease. With the company in funds once again, dividends could be paid and

Blandford Forum's Somerset & Dorset station, probably late 1950s. The town's first station was a temporary terminus opened in November 1860 at Blandford St Mary. (R.K.Blencowe)

72

The notice reads 'Blandford Forum for Bryanston School'. Ivatt class 2MT 2-6-2T no 41243 heads a passenger train, probably late 1950s. (R.K.Blencowe)

locomotives purchased. In 1885 the need for reversal at Wimborne was finally abolished when a cut-out was built between Broadstone and Corfe Mullen. Following formation of the new Joint Railway, rolling stock improved and traffic increased. Two years later the track northwards from Templecombe to Wincanton was doubled. Corfe Mullen to Blandford followed in 1901. Express trains commenced in the 1880s but the first Manchester-Bournemouth restaurant car train began on 1st October 1910. This remained unnamed until 1927 when it became the *Pines Express* running every weekday throughout the year.

When grouping came in 1923, the newly formed Southern Railway (SR) and the London, Midland & Scottish Railway (LMSR) became joint owners of the route between Bath and Broadstone. Several halts were built to offset road competition. A short spur to Blandford Army Camp which had only a two-year

At the former Blandford Forum station site, all that can be found is a buffer stop, a short section of track and a footbridge. Nearby on an estate of houses stands an old locomotive driving wheel. (Author)

existence (1919-1921) was dismantled in 1928. Until 1930 the S&D continued to operate as a separate railway but private motoring was on the increase and falling traffic made changes necessary. The SR took on the track and signalling while the LMSR assumed responsibility for traffic organisation, locomotives and most rolling stock.

In July 1933 the S&D line found an unexpected use when a farm was moved to Stalbridge by rail. According to *The Railway Magazine*, the entire equipment and stock of Brockwood Park Farm near West Meon was moved to Stalbridge in two Southern Railway trains. The stock included 50 sheep and lambs, 17 cows, 13 heifers and calves, 3 bulls, a goat plus a pony and foal, ferrets, dogs and pigeons. The only animal left behind was the farm cat which clearly took exception to the move.

When the Second World War came, services changed

dramatically. Instead of the expresses, the cross-country link proved its usefulness for the movement of equipment and war materials, much of it pulled by ageing class 7s. Here suddenly was a vital route between the industrial Midlands and the South Coast — a line that became very valuable during the build-up to D-Day. Little damage was caused by enemy bombing except that Templecombe station suffered in an air raid in September 1942. Blandford served as a military traffic centre and there was a temporary forces canteen on the up platform.

With petrol still in short supply after the war, passenger traffic became busy once again with holidaymakers flocking to the South and West. However, the general downward trend continued and, after nationalisation in 1948, considerable confusion followed. Initially the London Midland Region continued to operate the line from Bath while traffic supervision

Shillingstone station which overlooked the river Stour. The buildings were grander than might be expected for a rural station perhaps because the station was used by King Edward VII for visits to nearby Iwerne Minster House. (R.K.Blencowe)

The former Shillingstone station found close to an industrial estate and overlooking the river Stour. Apart from weeds and undergrowth the station seemed surprisingly intact following closure over 35 years ago. (Author)

came from the Southern Region at Southampton. Two years later the Western Region took over the line northwards from Cole while the Southern Region operated the line with locomotives loaned by the London Midland Region!

Further blows came in 1951 when the branch to Wells closed to all traffic and the link between Highbridge and the Bristol Channel at Burnham closed to passenger traffic (except for occasional excursions). In December 1952 the short branch to Bridgwater closed to passengers, surviving only until October 1954 for goods. Two years later, in September 1956, Charlton Marshall, Corfe Mullen, Spetisbury and Stourpaine & Durweston halts closed to cut further costs.

The greatest blow to the line came in September 1962 when it was announced that the well-known train the *Pines Express* (plus all through holiday expresses) was to be re-routed over the ex-

Sturminster Newton, August 1958. The station handled much cattle traffic in its time, also there was a siding serving a milk factory. (R.K.Blencowe)

GWR route via Oxford, Reading and Basingstoke. It was a sad day for the many who stood on 8th September to watch the last *Pines Express* hauled by 2-10-0 no 92220 *Evening Star* in first-class condition.

The end now seemed inevitable. Night freight trains were withdrawn by September 1964 with traffic diverted to other routes. By 1965 most freight facilities had gone and stations and signal boxes were being neglected. Also during 1965, Bournemouth West station closed temporarily in connection with electrification work, requiring S&D trains to terminate at Branksome or go on to Bournemouth Central. Bournemouth West never reopened as the Minister of Transport had meantime agreed to its closure.

A proposal to close the passenger service over the remainder of the S&D was announced in June 1964 to take effect in September 1964. This met with strong objections from the Transport Users' Consultative Committee (TUCC) and the

77

At Stalbridge this short stretch of track close to the ASD Yeovil factory is all that remains of the former railway station. (Author)

closure was delayed. Uncertainty gave way to falling morale and nothing further was heard until 10th September 1965 when the Minister's consent to closure was given. Once again there was a strong public reaction.

At a mass meeting of railwaymen held at Templecombe, in the presence of MPs and before television cameras, Western Region was accused of a 'cold-blooded, deliberate murder of the line, planned and carefully executed over a period of ten years before Dr Beeching's plan'. There could be no justification, the railwaymen considered, for Western Region deliberately letting the line run down over many years and then simply claiming that the line did not pay. Despite all efforts, closure was announced for 3rd January 1966, the same day that Western Region was to give up steam in favour of diesel locomotives.

Once again closure did not happen. In their (almost indecent) haste to close the S&D, proper arrangements to provide suitable alternative road transport had not been concluded. Instead of closure on 3rd January therefore, BR was compelled to provide an 'interim emergency service' consisting of, south of Temple-combe, five trains each way daily. This rather unsatisfactory situation lasted for just over two months with final closure occurring on 7th March 1966.

On the last day thousands of people lined the route with cameras and tape recorders to witness the end of the line. The last regular passenger train was double-headed with a light engine following. A coffin, traditional to such occasions, was put on board at Evercreech Junction. During the weekend, 'specials' were run, all packed with enthusiasts anxious not to miss a last ride.

Although the railway has completely gone, many reminders still exist. Blandford station has disappeared, its place taken by houses and an old folks' home. At the entrance to the home, a locomotive driving wheel stands, statue-like, as a memento of the past. A footbridge also remains plus its smoke deflector in addition to a very short section of track and a buffer stop. According to local hearsay Blandford station was haunted by a man who threw himself under a train in the 1930s. And, it is said, the ghost is still there today.

Shillingstone proved a delight to visit with its station building almost intact plus both its platforms. Overlooking the river Stour, it is sited by a small industrial estate that was once the goods yard. Not long before closure of the line, the station-master had a greenhouse behind the station building with produce often conveyed by 'private arrangement' with the train crews. There are hopes that steam trains may once again call at Shillingstone station. The North Dorset Railway Trust have plans to reopen the station and lease track 500 yards in each direction. They are seeking a 5-year lease and when the station is restored, it will serve as a small museum and a tea room. Much needs to be done since Shillingstone station has previously been used by a furniture maker and the bulk of the original interior has gone.

Sturminster Newton station has given way to a supermarket car park and the station at Stalbridge has been lost to the ASD

Yeovil factory. A section of track still exists across the road. Standing in a private garden at Templecombe on what was once the lower platform of 1887, it is possible to look through a railbridge under the Salisbury to Yeovil line where once S&D trains passed.

Finding old stations can prove quite difficult despite maps and street plans since so many town centres have changed beyond recognition. Seeking Broadstone during research, the author approached an elderly gentleman and asked if he knew where the old station was. 'Yes, I do', he replied quite emphatically — and then he walked away!

8

A Branch Line To Swanage

Wareham/Corfe Castle/Swanage

Swanage station, 4th June 1949, with ex-L&SWR M7 class 0-4-4T no 57 about to depart. (John H. Meredith)

First attempts to cross the Isle of Purbeck to reach Swanage by rail came with Bills presented to Parliament in 1847 and 1850 by the Southampton & Dorchester, proposing a branch from its line at Wareham. The primary intention was to serve stone quarries on the peninsula in addition to supplying quantities of clay deposits to various potteries. The Bills were not pursued.

Nothing further happened until 1861 when the L&SWR propsed a short branch from Wareham to the Creech Heath area to reach the clay deposits. On this occasion there was strong opposition from the people of Wareham who considered the route too close to their town. The Bill was dropped in 1862 although the workings at Creech were eventually to be served by an extensive narrow gauge system (2 ft 8 ins) reaching Wareham Harbour and, later, sidings at Furzebrook.

Travel remained difficult for the residents of Swanage. Although steamers called regularly from nearby resorts, the only route to Wareham, the nearest market town, was by carrier's cart available on just three days of the week. Since the fare was three shillings few could afford it and the cart (plus a daily boat from Poole — weather permitting) was generally used to bring in much-needed provisions rather than passengers. But for the energies and dedication of George Burt of Purbeck House, Swanage, it might have been some considerable time before trains reached the town — if ever.

Swanage's popularity as a seaside resort eventually became the main requirement for a railway and the absence of any such link became a serious handicap. On 18th July 1881 the Swanage Railway was authorised with a line via Worgret chosen and with one intermediary station at Corfe Castle. The authorised share capital was £90,000 and the L&SWR was to work the line with an option to purchase. Construction began on 5th May 1883 and within two years, on 5th May 1885, the line was ready for a Board of Trade inspection. A locomotive from Wareham and an L&SWR Director's Saloon were used for the purpose. The line met with approval and on 16th May a special train from Waterloo carrying company directors and various dignitaries ran to Swanage where they remained guests of George Burt at Purbeck House for a few days. To mark the opening, church bells rang, a band played and Burt addressed welcoming crowds.

The day regular services began, 20th May 1885, was marred by heavy rains and strong winds which stopped the Bournemouth steamers bringing in the hundreds of visitors expected. Yet despite the weather, the first train left Swanage at 7.30 am consisting of Beattie 2-4-0 well tank locomotive no 209 hauling five L&SWR four-wheeled carriages. So insistent had George

LMS class 2P 4-4-0 no 628 visits Swanage in the 1930s. The 50 ft turntable was cut up for scrap in 1967 when most of the station's tracks were lifted. (S.C.Townroe/R.K.Blencowe)

Burt and the local residents been that the first train should leave from Swanage, that the Beattie well tank locomotive had made the journey from Wareham station on a horse-drawn trailer! On board the train were the band and celebration committee and, while the official party had breakfast at Wareham's Red Lion hotel, the band paraded the streets. By the afternoon the weather had improved. Teas were provided for children at their schools and old folk in the Mowlem Institute and entertainments included a grand firework display in the evening.

During the early years of the line, five return passenger trains ran daily from Mondays to Saturdays only. This was because many considered that Sunday running 'disturbed the Lord's Day'. On 1st June 1885 goods services commenced from Corfe Castle and Swanage and in August 1885 the Swanage company, in accordance with the Act, asked the L&SWR to acquire the line. This it did, taking the necessary powers on 25th June 1886.

In this view of Corfe Castle station taken June 1966 from the castle remains, a passenger train is hauled by locomotive D6516. Corfe Castle station closed to regular passenger traffic in 1972. (R.K.Blencowe)

Trains for Swanage left the Southampton & Dorchester line at Worgret junction where there was an attractive L&SWR signal box. Before reaching Corfe Castle the track was carried over the Studland road (B3351) by an impressive four-arch viaduct built of Purbeck stone. The station itself was built within sight of the ruins of Corfe Castle.

Beyond Corfe Castle the railway continued via Harman's Cross more or less following the main A351 road to Swanage. The original Swanage station was constructed, like the Corfe Castle viaduct, from Purbeck stone and had a red tile roof. Facilities included a long platform together with a ticket office, staff room and an adjacent station-master's house. In addition there was a short length of canopy where passengers could shelter if necessary. A run-round loop was added by the L&SWR in 1897 to ease the operation of trains.

As holiday traffic increased during the 1930s, the Southern

84

Worgret junction, to the west of Wareham where branch line trains once left to cross the Isle of Purbeck to Swanage. Following talks between Swanage Railway and Network Rail, it is hoped that, by summer 2005, the connection may initially allow tracklaying trains to reach the restored Swanage branch. (Author)

Railway found it increasingly difficult to cope with the existing inadequate station. In 1937 it was agreed to upgrade both the station buildings and the signalling system to meet the demand. The goods shed was more than doubled in size and the station buildings were extended to their present size. All these changes were made with matching materials and consistent with the original 1885 structure. The new station included a parcels office, waiting hall, newsagent's shop, toilets and a lamp room. The wooden L&SWR signal box boasted 23 levers controlling all movements in the station area as well as providing a single line token instrument which was electrically linked to Corfe Castle.

By nationalisation in 1948 passenger services to Swanage had increased on weekdays to a dozen a day, mostly comprising a tank locomotive and a push-pull set of two or three coaches. During peak holiday periods, Bulleid Light Pacifics could be seen bringing through trains from Waterloo to the branch. But by the early 1960s traffic was dwindling and ageing M7 0-4-4Ts were replaced by BR Standard and ex-LMS Ivatt tank locomotives. These had to run round the coaches at each end, since they were not equipped for push-pull working. Towards the end of 1965 goods working ceased at Swanage and Corfe Castle. In 1966 'Hampshire' DEMUs took over from steam, not long before the end of Southern Region steam in July 1967. Yet such economies were not to save the line.

Although official closure of the branch was on 3rd January 1972, the actual final day of rail travel was 1st January. The train, comprising two three-coach 'Hampshire' DEMUs, left Wareham at 9.45 pm and finally returned from Swanage leaving at 10.15 pm to the accompaniment of detonators placed on the track. Special commemorative tickets were issued at 50p each.

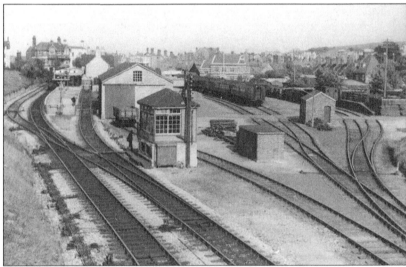

A general view of Swanage station on 4th June 1949. The station closed to goods traffic in October 1965 with sidings 5 and 6 (on the right) being lifted the following year. (John H. Meredith)

86

This picture taken from the bridge to the north of the station shows how the area has changed over the years with shops and buses taking over the former large goods yard. (Author)

The driver, 'Johnny' Walker from Bournemouth, was certainly familiar with the branch. Apart from regular workings, he had driven the last steam train out of Swanage in September 1966 and, in addition, had driven Merchant Navy Class Pacific no 35028 *Clan Line* on one of the last trains up the Somerset & Dorset on 6th March 1966.

After closure only the stretch from Worgret junction to Furzebrook sidings survived. Still in existence today, this is a freight-only line of less than three miles where One Train Working applies with a maximum speed of 20 mph. At Corfe Castle, a station used in the past by many thousands of passengers, the small shelter on the down platform was soon ivy-ridden. Swanage station too was in a derelict state. The whole area became run down and the station buildings were boarded up prior to demolition. No doubt many thought that passenger trains had gone for good across the Isle of Purbeck but they were to be proved very wrong.

In 1974, largely at the prompting of Swanage County Council member Brigadier R. Montague-Jones, the County Council bought the entire trackbed from Furzebrook to Northbrook Road bridge, Swanage. This was to be used to improve access to Purbeck since this was so poor, including possible use again as a railway although a road approach seemed more likely at the time. Crucially this kept the proverbial door open and prevented piecemeal development across the trackbed.

The re-opening of sections of the original Swanage branch proved difficult and prolonged. When the line closed in 1972 the impetus to save the line had been considerable, backed by a massive public protest. It had been announced there were plans to build a shop and hotel complex on Swanage station and also Dorset County Council intended to demolish a road bridge at Victoria Avenue, just out of the town centre. At about the same time the Isle of Purbeck Preservation Group, founded in 1969, gave up hope of buying and operating the line.

The situation worsened when tracklifting equipment entered the branch hauled by class 33 diesel locomotive no D6580. It was not long before a number of wayside huts had been collected and removed. On Saturday, 1st July 1972 it seemed that the situation had been saved when the Swanage Railway Society announced plans to buy the branch line in order to provide a rail service between Swanage and Wareham. As a result, BR's tracklifting operations were delayed but only after the Swanage Railway Society agreed an amount of interest on the scrap value of the track. There was considerable surprise therefore when, nine days after agreement had been reached, tracklifting began at Corfe Castle station by a Scunthorpe contractor — watched by BR officials! Telegrams were immediately sent to Peter Walker, the Minister of the Environment, Richard Marsh, the British Railways Board chairman, and the Swanage UDC asking them to intervene and stop the operation.

In his 'Railway World Special' book, *The Swanage Branch*, Andrew Wright relates the story of a Corfe Castle resident who

A sunny day at Swanage railway station September 2000. After closure of the line in 1966 steam returned to the branch on Bank Holiday Monday, 27th May 1985, being the beginnings of today's popular Swanage Railway. (Author)

remembered the occasion only too well. On that fateful day, he recalls watching Richard Marsh on television in a local interview stating quite definitely that tracklifting on the Swanage branch would not recommence, yet at the same time through his window he could see and hear the contractors not far away busily removing the track! By mid-August 1972, the track had been lifted completely except for the Furzebrook track north-wards to Worgret junction.

Further disasters followed. In March 1974, Swanage Town Council purchased the station site from BR but decided not to let it to the Swanage Railway Society which by now was greatly concerned at its deterioration. It was not long before the 1938 station canopy was stripped of its lead and glass, the long station platform at the western end was broken up and the rubble used to infill the trackbeds by the main platform. Where once trains had stood proudly, Hants & Dorset buses were parked.

Throughout all these activities the enthusiasts never once lost heart. Years of campaigning by the Swanage Railway Society followed and in July 1975 a referendum was held amongst Swanage residents. The result indicated strong support for the railway's return and, as a result, the Town Council granted a one-year lease of the station buildings to the society. However, no track could be laid except in the goods shed. When on 23rd September 1976 an ex-BR standard 4MT 2-6-4T locomotive no 80078, acquired from Barry scrapyard, was hauled through the streets of Swanage on its way to the station, the local residents knew the Society was serious.

The finding of large oil deposits at Wytch Farm, just north of Corfe Castle and the need for a rail terminal had already secured

Corfe Castle station, June 1966. Track lifting began very soon after closure in 1972 and the area became neglected. In 1983 the station buildings were leased to Eastpoint Ltd, an electronics company, and one of its directors, Les Hayward, restored them to their former glory. (R.K.Blencowe)

Corfe Castle station today as passengers await a train back to Swanage after having spent time in the village. Corfe Castle is recalled by many as 'Casterbridge' as portrayed in the TV film 'The Mayor of Casterbridge'. (Author)

the future of the stretch of track from Worgret junction to Furzebrook. At Swanage the Town Council agreed a Statement of Intent concerning the rebuilding of the branch line to link with BR. Approval was granted for more tracklaying, more rolling stock arrived and the 1938 station canopy was fully restored. In February 1979 the Swanage Railway Co was formed and, on 15th May 1979, Dorset County Council finally agreed to the laying of track and the operation of a service over one mile between Swanage and Herston. Almost two years later in February 1981, the council agreed a lease on a further section from Herston to Harman's Cross, some three miles from Swanage.

It was a proud moment for all concerned when, on Good Friday, 20th April 1984, the first public steam train reached Herston from Swanage. Just over a year later there was another occasion to celebrate. On Bank Holiday Monday, 27th May 1985,

91

a special train called the 'Centenarian', double-headed with Hunslet 0-6-0 ST *Cunarder* of 1931 and Hawthorn Leslie 0-6-0 ST *Linda* of 1938, travelled over this restored mile after a re-enactment of the original opening ceremony which had taken place one hundred years previously.

Final success was achieved on 24th July 1986 when the Dorset County Council voted unanimously that the Swanage Railway should be permitted to re-open the section between Harman's Cross, Corfe Castle and Furzebrook. At last connections with Wareham could be envisaged and through trains reaching Swanage from Waterloo or Bournemouth might one day be a possibility.

The Swanage Railway ran its first passenger train to reach Harman's Cross on Saturday, 3rd December 1988, just 24 hours after gaining Railway Inspectorate approval to use the line. Only

'257 Squadron' 4-6-2 locomotive no 34072 built 1948 runs round coaches at Swanage on Sunday, 17th September 2000 before departing for Norden at 1400 hrs. (Author)

A slightly amended warning notice at Swanage station usefully serves its purpose by forsaking the L&SWR for the SR (Swanage Railway). (Author)

a week earlier, Tarmac Roadstone helped complete the new six-coach platform by donating and laying free of charge the surface asphalt. A seven-man Tarmac gang agreed to work without wages on a Saturday to complete the job. The first train comprised six coaches double-headed by ex-Midland Railway 0-6-0T no 41708 and ex-LMS *Jinty* 0-6-0T no 47383.

Today, regular train services operate throughout most of the year with stops at Herston (by request), Harman's Cross, Corfe Castle and Norden. Trains can pass on a loop at Harman's Cross while at Corfe Castle visitors can enjoy the high standard of this beautifully restored Victorian station. Since 1983 the station building had been occupied by Eastpoint Ltd, an electronics company, which has a connection with the branch. The grand-father of one of Eastpoint's founder-directors was at one time a station-master at Corfe Castle station. When Eastpoint Ltd left the Corfe Castle premises in 1992, the way was clear for the

Trains pass at Harman's Cross on the Swanage Railway, 17th September 2000. The Swanage bound train is headed by ex-BR locomotive 2-6-4T and the train on the far platform by '257 Squadron' ex-SR locomotive no 34702. (Jackie Oppitz)

Swanage Railway to use the main buildings as well as the platform. At Norden rail trips can begin or end adjacent to an area where car or coach parking is not a problem and where regular bus services connect with Wareham on train operating days.

The main streets of Corfe Castle had a claim to fame some years ago when they became the centrepiece for the television adaptaion of Thomas Hardy's *The Mayor of Casterbridge*. To provide authenticity for the occasion, telephone wires and television aerials were removed and extra houses were produced in plastic. A finishing touch to transform the area into the county town of Casterbridge (Dorchester) was a replica of Dorchester's town pump created in glass fibre. Local folk also contributed.

94

The first London to Swanage steam train since 1967 runs into Corfe Castle station with the 'Royal Wessex' excursion on Saturday, 2nd May 2009, with Bulleid Pacific class steam locomotive No. 34067 'Tangmere' at its head. Simmering to the left is fellow Battle of Britain class Bulleid Pacific No. 34070 'Manston' on a Swanage to Norden Park & Ride train. (Photograph courtesy of Andrew P. M. Wright)

Cottage owners filled their gardens with old-world flowers such as fuchsias, hollyhocks and snapdragons.

There is no doubt that, despite the disappointments and the struggles over the past 40 years, the Swanage Railway still has further great prospects ahead. After a link with Worgret Junction was achieved in 2007, the first diesel and excursion trains from London to Swanage, organised by train charter companies, ran in April and May 2009.

In February 2013, the Swanage Railway was awarded a 1.47 million pound grant from the Government's Coastal Communities Fund to provide signalling and track upgrade work to enable a test train service from Swanage to Wareham. This is due to begin in September 2015. The railway has indeed made great strides since February 1979 when the Swanage Railway Company was formed.

9
Lines Around Weymouth

Weymouth Quay Branch
Weymouth/Portland/Easton
Upwey Junction/Portesham/Abbotsbury

Passenger trains first reached Weymouth Quay in August 1889, the date coinciding with the GWR take-over of the Channel Islands packet service. This c1910 picture shows Weymouth Quay and the nearby Pavilion Theatre, then showing 'Oh Susannah'. (Lens of Sutton)

Weymouth Quay Branch

A short branch between Weymouth and Weymouth Quay (known as the Weymouth Harbour Tramway) opened in 1874.

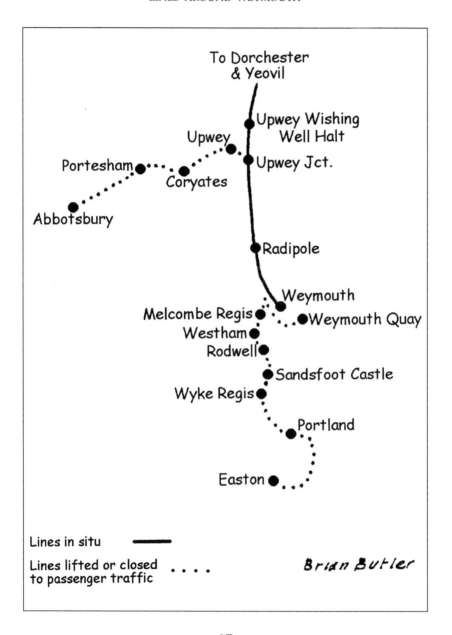

To Dorchester
& Yeovil

Upwey Wishing
Well Halt

Upwey

Portesham

Coryates

Upwey Jct.

Abbotsbury

Radipole

Weymouth

Melcombe Regis

Weymouth Quay

Westham

Rodwell

Sandsfoot Castle

Wyke Regis

Portland

Easton

Lines in situ

Lines lifted or closed
to passenger traffic

Brian Butler

Former Bristol & Exeter Railway locomotive 0-6-0T no 1376 heads a passenger set through the streets of Weymouth, 1910. The short branch to the Quay closed to freight in 1972 and passenger trains lasted until 1987. (R.K.Blencowe)

It was built initially for goods and horse traction was used. GWR lines in the area had hitherto been opened as broad gauge but they were converted to standard gauge at the same time the Harbour Tramway opened so the branch to the Quay opened as standard gauge track.

As traffic increased the suggestion was made that a small engine should be employed. In 1878 members of Weymouth corporation were given a trial run in a carriage hauled by a small steam locomotive travelling at about four miles an hour. The council members considered such traction might be dangerous to the public so during the journey one member suddenly got in front of the engine to see how quickly it could stop. Fortunately it stopped in time with the engine brought up almost within its own length. Suitably reassured, the council at its next meeting agreed locomotives could be used.

Weymouth Quay, September 2000. The last regular passenger train left the Quay on 27th September 1987 with only specials covering the line after that date. (Author)

On 4th August 1889 the Weymouth Quay line was opened to passenger traffic, coinciding with the GWR takeover of the Channel Islands packet service. Traffic increased considerably as well as freight which included the import of flowers, new potatoes and tomatoes. In the 1930s, as business improved, the 30 ft wide pier was replaced by one of 100 ft and the Quay platform was considerably enlarged. In 1938 the Quay was widened so that coaches could negotiate Ferry's Corner without the need for special extra-length couplings.

Each engine was required to have a bell which was rung continuously by the fireman along the route when the train was in motion. In addition a shunter-in-charge had to have in his possession a guard's whistle, a set of flags and, for use at night, a hand lamp. It was his job to see that the line in front of the train was clear and he had to warn everyone of its approach either by red flag or red lamp. A speed limit of 4 mph was imposed.

The last passenger train to reach Weymouth Quay ran on 27th September 1987 and only specials have covered the line since that date. When visited in the year 2000, the tracks to the quay were still in evidence. Even so, there must be many who still recall the sight of the steam locomotive slowly making its way through Weymouth's streets preceded by a shunter waving his red flag.

Weymouth/Portland/Easton

The Isle of Portland, referred to by Thomas Hardy as 'the Gibraltar of Wessex', is connected to the mainland only by the

Easton station, the terminus of the branch on the Isle of Portland. The branch closed in 1952 but freight traffic lasted until 1965. In this August 1960 photograph an ex-GWR 57XX class 0-6-0 passenger traffic no 3737 heads an RCTS special. (R.K.Blencowe)

A train hauled by tank locomotive no 233 enters Melcombe Regis on 4th June 1949. Note the anti-invasion defences still in existence on the right. (John H. Meredith)

easterly end of Chesil Beach. The Portland area comprises a solid block of limestone and for hundreds of years it has been extensively quarried. Construction of the Weymouth & Portland Railway began at the end of 1862 following an agreement that the line should be worked jointly by the GWR and the L&SWR. Work was completed by April 1864 but the opening had to be postponed while timber viaducts were strengthened to meet Board of Trade requirements and there were also disagreements over the accommodation of Portland trains at Weymouth station. Eventually on 16th October 1865 the line opened. It was of mixed gauge to allow trains from both companies although from June 1874 the narrow gauge became standard. An intermediate station opened at Rodwell in June 1870.

In 1878 a line of just over a mile in length was completed from a junction with the Weymouth & Portland Railway to the breakwater entrance near the South Ship Channel. Known as the

Ex-Adams 02 class 0-4-4T no 30179 heads the 12.53 pm passenger train as it leaves Westham Halt bound for Portland in March 1952. (B.Knowlman/ R.K.Blencowe)

'Admiralty' line (or by some the Breakwater line) it was used mainly for coal traffic and worked by the GWR and L&SWR jointly at the Admiralty's expense.

In 1867 a quite separate company, the Easton & Church Hope Railway (E&CHR), was incorporated. The basic intention was to provide broad gauge rail transport for stone from the centre of the island to a pier to be built at Church Hope Cove (later known as Church Ope Cove). The line involved two reversals and a 1 in 8 cable-worked incline but it was never concluded. In 1883 the idea was abandoned and instead the E&CHR proposed an extension to join the Weymouth & Portland Railway which included running powers over the Admiralty line. This was approved in 1884 but it was 1900 before a line from Portland was opened. Much of the track had to be built through solid rock to a new station at Easton and at first only goods traffic was permitted. The Board of Trade refused to allow passenger traffic until the Admiralty line had been brought up to a satisfactory standard, a cost which the E&CHR grudgingly had to bear after the Admiralty had terminated its contract with the GWR and the L&SWR. Passenger traffic started on 1st September 1902 with a new station opened at Portland and with the original station becoming a goods depot. The Portland branch now worked as a continuous line from Weymouth through to Easton but the Weymouth & Portland and the Easton & Church Hope Railways kept their independence right through to nationalisation.

In 1908 when it became necessary to replace the old wooden viaduct over the Backwater adjacent to Weymouth station, the opportunity was taken to reclaim land on which a separate branch station was built, to be called Melcombe Regis. This opened in 1909 with halts being opened at Westham and Wyke Regis coinciding with the introduction of L&SWR rail motor services. Sandsfoot Castle Halt, about a mile from Weymouth's

Ex-L&SWR Adams 02 class 0-4-4Ts nos 30179 and 30197 double-head a passenger train as it enters Portland in March 1952, two days before the station's closure to passenger traffic. (B.Knowlman/R.K.Blencowe)

A 'Southern Counties Enterprise' special visits Easton on 25th August 1963. (John H. Meredith)

town centre, opened in August 1932 in an attempt to capture some of the traffic that was by now drifting onto the roads.

There was excitement in the 1930s when the Royal Train arrived at Portland on a very stormy night. King Edward VIII travelled from London straight from a Remembrance ceremony at the Albert Hall to spend two days with his fleet but at the time of arrival the sea was coming over Chesil Beach with a vengeance. It was not long before the King was asleep in the Royal Train in the goods yard but the coach was soon up to its floorboards in water. All traffic was stopped and the King was marooned. Fortunately by the time the train was due to pull out the water had subsided.

As the number of passengers fell and as Portland's population dwindled due to reduced activity by the Navy, so bus services were able to compete effectively. During the Second World War, Easton was served during the summer only and on 3rd March 1952 passenger services were withdrawn throughout. Freight

Easton station building in February 1952, three weeks before closure. During the Second World War from 1941 to 1944 passenger services ran in the summer months only. (John H. Meredith)

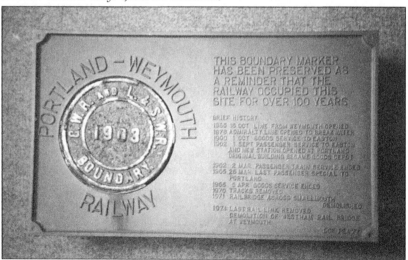

The site of Portland station has become the Royal Naval Air Station HMS Osprey. A plaque to recall the railway is currently in storage pending relocation. (Photograph courtesy of HMS Osprey)

105

The site of Easton station is today Ladymead Hall, a residence for elderly people. Just beyond the site is this roadbridge which once spanned the end of the platform. (Author)

lasted at Portland and Easton until 5th April 1965 and by 1970 the tracks had been removed. The last rail link from Weymouth to Portland went in 1974 when Westham rail bridge at Weymouth was demolished.

The site of Portland station today is occupied by the Royal Naval Air Station HMS *Osprey*. Elsewhere there is still evidence of where the track existed at many places but Easton station has been completely demolished. Its place has been taken by an old peoples' residence called 'Ladymead Hall'.

Upwey Junction/Portesham/Abbotsbury

There is a period in Abbotsbury's history which many will recall. For almost 70 years steam trains chugged along a single track

A branch to Abbotsbury was built initially to carry stone deposits from Portesham and iron ore from Abbotsbury but results proved disappointing. This picture of Abbotsbury station showing GWR 14XX class 0-4-2T no 1467 with motor carriage 165 was taken in June 1949. (John H. Meredith)

from Upwey Junction on the main Dorchester to Weymouth line to reach the village. The railway was initially built to exploit stone deposits at Portesham and iron ore at Abbotsbury, but as time passed results proved disappointing. The line was to eventually depend on passenger traffic, mostly to the nearby Swannery behind Chesil Bank, for its existence.

The Abbotsbury Railway was first proposed in 1872 but the Bill was withdrawn the following year because of opposition from an influential local landowner. A fresh application to Parliament was made in time for the 1876/7 session and this received Royal Assent on 6th August 1877. Difficulty in raising capital led to delays and at one stage in 1881 work ceased altogether and the company had to apply for an extension of time plus a slight deviation of route. The latter had become necessary to defeat a speculator who had bought land and then

107

Upwey, one of the three intermediate stations on the Abbotsbury branch. Initially known as Broadway, in June 1891 it was renamed Broadwey in order to avoid confusion with Broadway in Worcestershire. In 1913 it was renamed Upwey since confusion still existed. (F.A.Blencowe/R.K.Blencowe)

demanded extortionate terms. On 9th November 1885 the line was finally opened. In all it had taken eight years to construct 6 miles of track. It was built to a standard gauge width since the main line had already been converted from broad gauge.

At one stage the railway planners ambitiously hoped to continue beyond Abbotsbury to Axminster to form a link with Plymouth and the West. Despite such a grandiose idea, the 6 mile branch never really reached any importance. It was worked by the GWR which had found it necessary to contribute £10,000 towards the cost of completion. There were intermediate stations at Broadway and Portesham. All three stations on the branch were of stone construction having been built by Mr Edwin Snook, a local contractor. In June 1891 Broadway was renamed Broadwey in order to avoid confusion with Broadway in Worcestershire. In 1913 it was renamed Upwey (as distinct from

GWR Portesham station on the Abbotsbury branch in 1958, six years after closure of the line. The station became a private dwelling appropriately called 'Sleepers'. (Stations UK)

Upwey Junction on the main line) since confusion still existed.

The branch left the main Weymouth line at Upwey Junction. The Abbotsbury line platform was on a slightly lower level and linked by steps to the main-line platform since the branch was already commencing a downhill westward curve towards its own Upwey station. In 1896 the branch was taken over by the GWR. When the GWR introduced steam rail motors, a new halt was opened at Coryates in 1906. It comprised a small wooden platform plus a mere corrugated iron shelter. It was added to encourage local passenger traffic yet, sited remote from any human habitation, it is doubted that it contributed much to the line.

When the line began there were four trains each way daily but by 1902 this had risen to five. The main traffic consisted of milk and agricultural produce plus, during the summer season, mackerel caught from Chesil Beach. During the 1930s milk

109

Portesham station building and platform photographed almost 50 years after closure. It currently serves as a holiday cottage. (Author)

Abbotsbury station has gone but a goods shed and loading gauge can still be found. Stones from the former station building were used to build a wall round a private bungalow on the site. (Author)

traffic improved sufficiently to justify a small wooden platform at Friar Waddon. As passenger traffic continued to increase, railway camping coaches were introduced in 1935 at Abbotsbury and Portesham and during the following year at Upwey. The coaches were popular but they could only be used by holiday-makers arriving by rail. During the winter months they were stored at Swindon where they were repainted to the high standards for which the GWR was well known. When war broke out in 1939 they were removed for the last time.

In the autumn of 1952 closure notices were posted at stations along the line. Despite protests, the last train ran on 29th November 1952 on a wet and windy night. Before it left Abbotsbury, a wreath was placed on the smokebox of the push-pull engine, 0-4-2T (ex-GWR) 1400 class no 1453, with the inscription, 'In loving memory of the Abbotsbury Railway, 1885-1952, ever faithful, ever sure, from Abbotsbury Parish Council'. As the train pulled out, about 50 villagers braving the driving rain stood holding hands singing *Auld Lang Syne* illuminated by the station's oil lamps. Probably the oldest passenger was Mr A.E. Snook, well into his eighties, the son of Mr Edwin Snook who had built the original branch stations. The son had the distinction of having travelled on the first as well as the last train over the line.

At Portesham the station became a private dwelling appro-priately called 'Sleepers'. Here the platform and building remain intact plus a short section of picket fencing. At Abbotsbury the station building has gone although the platform edge can still be determined. The local stone that once comprised the building has been used for a wall around a private bungalow built on the site. Yet nearby the goods shed plus a loading gauge remain although the ground frames, the signal box and the water tower have gone. Fortunately for posterity, much of the old railway line has been preserved as a footpath.

When the branch closed in 1952 the feelings of many local folk were summed up by a resident who said, 'Now we be back to where we was avore they made the line'.

10
A GWR Line From Bath To Weymouth

Yeovil/Dorchester/Weymouth

A mixed train passes through Upwey Junction, c1935. The station, between Dorchester and Weymouth, also served the short branch line to Abbotsbury. (Stations UK)

From incorporation to opening, the broad gauge Wilts, Somerset & Weymouth Railway (WS&WR) took twelve years to complete. It began during the time of 'railway mania' when too many lines were chasing too little capital. Loans became unobtainable and companies were being obliged to cut back on existing contracts. At one stage during 1848 work stopped completely.

Yetminster, seen here in 1959, on the GWR line from Yeovil to Weymouth has today been badly downgraded since it opened in 1857. The line has been singled and the original platform buildings and signal box have gone. (Stations UK)

The WS&WR, incorporated on 30th June 1845, was authorised to build a railway from Thingley junction, on the GWR line from Bath to Chippenham, to Salisbury. Numerous branches were planned including a line via Yeovil to Dorchester and Weymouth. Less than a month later the standard gauge Southampton & Dorchester (L&SWR from 1848) obtained powers to proceed with its own line, with the Act including running powers over the WS&WR Dorchester to Weymouth section. Both Acts took into account a mixed gauge junction at Dorchester plus the need for mixed gauge track between Dorchester and Weymouth.

In 1850 the GWR reluctantly assumed responsibility for the cash-stricken WS&WR line and work restarted. Progress remained slow and an extension of the original Parliamentary powers, granted for seven years, became necessary in 1852. Public concern over delays in reaching Weymouth increased and

113

Evershot, photographed 1939, which closed to freight traffic in 1964 and to passengers in 1966. The station was situated at a height of 500 ft above sea level. (Stations UK)

Maiden Newton station on the line (formerly GWR) from Bath to Weymouth. On the right the former bay for trains to Bridport. (Author)

writs were issued. A further extension in time was agreed by Parliament in 1854 with a clause stipulating completion to Weymouth within two years. The GWR was becoming increasingly anxious that the line to the coast would be lost completely to the L&SWR. Work progressed and finally, on 20th January 1857, the GWR line to Weymouth was completed. L&SWR services from the Southampton and Dorchester line began on the same day.

Passengers were few on the first GWR train to leave Weymouth although there were numerous spectators despite the wintry weather. It left at 6.15 am and was hauled by 2-4-0 locomotive *Otho*. The train arrived exactly on time at Yeovil at 7.10 am, an event described by the *Southern Times* as '... an evidence of punctuality which, in a first attempt, is rather extraordinary'.

Grimstone and Frampton between Dorchester West and Maiden Newton was originally called just Frampton, and then just Grimstone. After closure the site became a depot for an oil company. (Stations UK)

Dorchester West station, c1930, showing signs of neglect. The line was opened as broad gauge in January 1857 by the Wilts, Somerset & Weymouth Railway which was taken over by the GWR in 1850. (Stations UK)

Celebrations were delayed somewhat, partly because the GWR had given short notice of its intentions. When festivities were eventually held a week later on 27th January, they were enjoyed by all. The day was declared a public holiday, the streets were decorated and there was a grand procession from the town hall to the station which included the mayor and his corporation and which was headed by the band of the 15th Hussars. Later a dinner was held at the Royal Hotel and a ball took place at the Victoria Hotel. The GWR made available 300 free rides from Weymouth to Yeovil.

Intermediate stations in Dorset were at Yetminster, Evershot, Maiden Newton, Frampton (later Grimstone and Frampton) and Dorchester (Dorchester West from September 1949). Between Weymouth and Dorchester the track was double but northwards towards Yeovil it was single. The section between Evershot and Yeovil was doubled in 1858. The GWR ran six trains daily to

116

Dorchester West station looking southwards showing a truncated track off to the left. Goods sidings once existed which allowed interchange of GWR/ L&SWR goods traffic between Dorchester West and Dorchester South. (Author)

Weymouth and the L&SWR ran five down and seven up. The L&SWR's distance to London was 21 miles shorter than the GWR's but there was little difference in timing. Both routes proved immediately popular.

Cheap excursions to Weymouth became a regular feature. These were well patronised, bringing visitors to the resort from places such as London, Bath or Bristol. During August 1861 one GWR excursion train alone consisted of 22 carriages and brought 850 passengers to the town, many of them described as 'working class' people. The number of lodging houses rose continually to accommodate visitors. Many of the employees from the GWR Swindon Works and their families made for Weymouth with the majority being cared for by, we are told, the 'poorer type of seaside landlady'.

On 26th August 1862 there was a serious yet spectacular

117

A DMU awaits departure to Bristol Temple Meads at Upwey station, formerly Upwey Junction. To the north is 819 yard Bincombe tunnel which cuts through Ridgeway Hill. (Author)

accident at Weymouth when the 7.20 pm train from Chippenham ran out of control when descending Upwey bank. The fireman jumped off before the engine, 2-4-0 *Victoria,* reached the buffers, injuring himself by hitting one of the roof supports. The locomotive smashed through the buffer stops at Weymouth to career on across King Street, coming to rest just short of the Somerset Hotel. The incident gave rise to a song of the day with the refrain 'Victoria in the gin-shop'.

Meantime Brunel's broad gauge system of 7 ft 0¼ ins was losing ground against George Stephenson's standard gauge of 4 ft 8½ ins which was being accepted by other railways. In June 1874 therefore it was decided to convert the WS&WR to standard gauge, a formidable task that was carried out in a remarkably record time. The line from Dorchester to Weymouth already accommodated both gauges, so initially it was only necessary to

118

Tank locomotive no 4133 runs bunker first through Radipole Halt (between Upwey Junction and Weymouth) bound for Weymouth Motive Power Depot, August 1960. (F.A.Blencowe/R.K.Blencowe)

remove the outer rail. Northwards from Dorchester there was much that needed to be done. Yet the entire task of 'narrowing' 110 miles of track was completed in only five days.

In the 1960s the line escaped the Beeching cuts and of course it exists today. Travelling the route southwards from Yeovil Pen Mill, the first station is Thornford. Opened in March 1936 as Thornford Bridge Halt, it lost its halt status in 1969 and was renamed Thornford in May 1974. Originally when the track was doubled the station had staggered standard timber-frame platforms but these were replaced by a concrete platform following line singling in 1968, the platform and shelter inherited from Cattistock Halt which closed in 1966.

Yetminster station has been badly downgraded, having lost its original building and canopy, its signal box and its down line. A bus stop type shelter provides the only cover and intending passengers must be vigilant since below the station nameplate is

119

the notice, 'Trains stop here on request. Please signal clearly to the Driver'.

Chetnole Halt, like Thornford, originally had staggered platforms and these were replaced by a concrete platform and shelter, also from Cattistock. Beyond the 308 yard long Evershot tunnel, came Evershot station which closed completely on 3rd October 1966. It was situated at a height of about 500 ft above sea level at the summit of the line. Southwards from Evershot, the line descends along the valley of the river Frome and, during wartime, ammunition trains were restricted in load down Evershot Bank towards Weymouth and Portland.

Cattistock Halt opened in 1931 and was rebuilt with concrete sections following the introduction of DMU services in 1959. Like others along the line, insufficient use caused its closure in October 1966 with, as mentioned earlier, its structures re-assembled elsewhere. A short distance to the south comes

In 1989 the Daily Telegraph *described Dorchester West station (seen here 1953) as 'one of the country's worst railway stations with graffiti everywhere and decaying walls'. To the south of Dorchester West the line is joined by tracks from Bournemouth. (Stations UK)*

Dorchester West station which retains some of its original buildings. The main building became the Lee Palace Restaurant in 2000, serving Peking food. Nearby buildings such as Isambard Court and G.W. Court recall Brunel days. (Author)

Maiden Newton which until 1975 included a terminal bay for the Bridport branch. Today the bay exists but the track has gone and the covered way at the station building end has been demolished. The earlier lattice footbridge at Maiden Newton across the main tracks has been replaced by a plain concrete construction.

Grimstone and Frampton station was originally known as just Frampton. However, the locals remained undecided and in 1857 it was decided to change it to Grimstone. One year later it acquired joint names. In Frampton, houses still exist which accommodated the men who came to build the railway in the late 1840s. After closure the station was completely demolished to become a site for an oil company. Next came Bradford Peverell and Stratton Halt which closed in 1966.

121

Dorchester West was described in its time as 'a fine station by Ritson with a broad hipped roof extending outwards to form awnings on all sides' although today the years have taken their toll. Looking southwards from the station platform it is possible to see where a track once led to Dorchester South which made possible the interchange of GWR/L&SWR goods.

Beyond Dorchester came Monkton and Came Halt which opened in 1905 as Came Bridge Halt to serve nearby golf courses as well as the two villages. The halt closed in 1957. After the 814 yard Bincombe tunnel, came Upwey Wishing Well Halt which also opened in 1905. Today the halt may be gone (it closed in 1957) but the wishing well is still there. To be found just off the B3159 near Upwey village it has been visited through the years by Royalty and tourists alike, at a spot where the river Wey rises.

Upwey station opened on 21st June 1871 following a public subscription to the GWR towards the expense. This closed in 1886 when Upwey Junction opened a short distance to the south following the opening of the Abbotsbury Railway. Yet Upwey's first station is not forgotten. Although completely demolished, Old Station Road can be located and an older building nearby was once known as Station Cafe. The last station before Weymouth was Radipole which opened as Radipole Halt in 1905. This survived a closure threat during 1983 but it finally officially closed on 6th February 1984.

Weymouth, a timber-built station, was constructed by T. Dodson of Weymouth for approximately £10,000. In 1939 the glass was removed from the glazed end screens as an air raid precaution and in March 1951 the overall roof was taken away. As traffic increased so the platforms were lengthened. In April 1957 a new platform 950 ft in length came into use, able to accommodate a 14-coach train and locomotive. Since May 1988 pride of place has been given to the 100 mph air-conditioned Wessex Electrics following electrification of the final stretch from Bournemouth to Weymouth.

This chapter concludes with a reference back to Dorchester West which during the 1980s suffered badly from vandalism and graffiti. Below is part of a poem written by Kenneth Leigh (after the style of Betjeman) published in the *Daily Telegraph* on 10th February 1989:

> Built by Brunel in the glorious age
> Of Victorian power and the great broad gauge,
> Rusted it stands with leprous wall
> Daubed with graffiti, but still recalls
> The grandeur that was steam.

11
To Bridport And West Bay

Maiden Newton/Bridport/West Bay

Bridport station, c1910. After closure in 1975 the site in St Andrew's Road was for a time occupied by Humphrey's Garden Centre but by the year 2000 it had become a Co-op Pioneer Supermarket. (Stations UK)

There must have been much rejoicing in the town of Bridport when the ceremony of cutting the first sod was held at Loders on 15th June 1855 for a broad gauge line to be built from Maiden Newton to Bridport. It was cut by Joseph Gundry who had been elected chairman of the newly established Bridport Railway.

Previously there had been a great deal of dissatisfaction in the town. Repeated proposals to establish a rail link had come from

A train headed by ex-GWR 57XX class 0-6-0PT no 4689 waits at Maiden Newton to leave for Bridport on 17th August 1960. The branch closed in 1975. (F.A.Blencowe/R.K.Blencowe)

various quarters but none of these had materialised. In 1845 the Wilts, Somerset & Weymouth Railway (WS&WR) had included a line to Bridport in its plans but after years of delays and financial problems the idea had been dropped. There were also schemes to include the town in the 'race' to reach Exeter but again these failed. Finally the townsfolk of Bridport decided that if they wanted a railway of their own, they would have to build it themselves. The Bridport Railway was incorporated on 5th May 1855.

At this stage the L&SWR proposed a narrow gauge line from Dorchester to Exeter through Bridport, a move which upset the Bridport Railway chairman sufficiently to warrant a letter to *The Times*. The chairman said he thought this was a clear case of 'unnecessary competition with existing and authorised lines of railway'. When a L&SWR line between Yeovil and Axminster was agreed by Parliament in May 1856, the idea for a coast route via Bridport was dropped.

Intermediate stations on the proposed Bridport branch were planned at Toller (Toller Porcorum) and Powerstock. The first was postponed because of plans for a new road in the area but a tender to build Powerstock (named Poorstock until about 1862) was accepted at a cost of £260 10s 0d. A petition was received from the people of Loders requesting a station, but this was never built even though the line almost passed through the village.

There were problems during construction, particularly with earth-slips at Witherstone cutting between Toller and Power-stock. In addition the company was running short of cash and for a time the line's future was in jeopardy. Eventually the company's remaining unsold shares were taken up and, although work continued, economies were necessary. An offer by the Bridport Gas Company to supply gas to Bridport station

Bridport station in the 1920s. When opened in 1857 the tracks were broad gauge but the branch was converted to narrow gauge in 1874. The work was completed in just three days. (S.V.Blencowe/R.K.Blencowe)

Bridport East Street, c1930, an intermediate station on the short extension to West Bay. After the branch had opened it was at one time thought that East Street might become Bridport's main station but this did not happen. (Stations UK)

for £60, provided the railway agreed to burn 16 lamps, was declined. Instead it was agreed that naphtha lamps, as used by the GWR, would be installed at Bridport and Powerstock stations at 6s 8d per month.

At last, on Thursday, 12th November 1857, the great day came. The weather was good and there were crowds at Bridport station to see the first train leave for Maiden Newton at 8.15 am. The locomotive carried a flag at each corner and, all along the nine mile route, people turned out to watch. The locomotives, rolling stock and staff were all supplied by the GWR. The following day, 17th November, was declared a public holiday. Shops were closed and local folk celebrated the event. A banquet was held at the Bull Hotel in Bridport's East Street with many notable visitors present. Two local MPs and two Bridport Railway Company directors arrived by carriage preceded by the Bridport Band.

127

Bridport West Bay station in the 1930s. When the West Bay extension opened in 1884 it was hoped the area would become a major resort but the railway company was disappointed. (S.V.Blencowe/R.K.Blencowe)

At first there were five trains each way on Monday to Saturday with none on Sundays. By the end of the year this had been reduced to four trains each way. There was an unusual arrangement at Maiden Newton where there was no run-round loop. In order to reverse the train for the journey back to Bridport, the engine had to push the coaches from the bay platform up a 'gravity siding' and then shunt back to the branch approach. The coaches could then be rolled back into the platform and the engine rejoined.

Over the next few years difficulties continued. Money was short and there were problems in raising further capital. There were more earth slippages at Witherstone cutting. On 31st March 1862, Toller station, postponed from 1857, was opened quite close to the village. There was a short festive gathering to celebrate the occasion with numerous local dignitaries present.

In June 1874, in common with the line from Yeovil to

Dorchester, the Bridport branch was converted from broad to standard gauge. The last broad gauge locomotive left the branch late on Thursday, 18th June, and the line was completely closed for three days. The change went well and within three days standard gauge locomotives and rolling stock were reaching Bridport. Normal service resumed on Monday, 22nd June.

The next event of importance came in July 1879 when a Bill was authorised for an extension from Bridport to the harbour with the GWR agreeing to contribute approximately £12,000 towards the cost of its construction. The extension was opened on 31st March 1884. There was an intermediate station at East Street where a thatched cottage was purchased and converted to a station-master's house, booking office and waiting room to save expense. One may wonder how the thatch survived the many sparks that flew from the locomotives' chimneys!

West Bay station building has been restored from a derelict state to become a Tourist Information Bureau and Visitor Centre. The two carriages on a short stretch of line have been loaned by the Swanage Railway. (Author)

129

A diesel railcar approaches Powerstock (Poorstock until about 1862) on the Bridport branch. When the line opened in 1857 the single platform station cost £260 10s 0d to build. (R.K.Blencowe)

The importance of Bridport Harbour dwindled over the years so the railway authorities decided to call their station West Bay in the hope that the area would develop into a major seaside resort. An esplanade was envisaged together with a sea wall to include walks and drives. Plans were considered for the building of numerous modern residences. The railway company asked, 'Why should West Bay not rival Bournemouth in the future?'

The opening to West Bay was celebrated in style with flags and bunting on buildings in East Street and South Street. There was a procession, many shops closed and an arch was erected near East Street station decorated with flags and greenery and carrying the words 'Success to the Railway' on one side and 'Prosperity to West Bay' on the other. As was to be expected, the first train carried a large number of people and, later in the day, 1,100 Sunday School children were given a ride to West Bay and each given a bun and an orange. At the terminus, bad weather prevented the children from leaving the station so they were taken straight back to Bridport. Surely it must have needed much patience on the teachers' part to control 1,100 frustrated children – all with sticky fingers!

History tells us of course that the major resort did not come about but plans were considered to make East Street the main station. In 1887 Bridport station was renamed Bridport Bradpole Road but in 1892 it was decided to retain Bradpole Road as the main station. In 1894 improvements were carried out when the platform was lengthened and a canopy fitted. A new platform plus canopy was built on the down side and a new signal box was constructed. On 1st July 1901 the branch was taken over entirely by the GWR and in 1902 the name of Bridport was restored. In addition the thatched station building at East Street was replaced with a new GWR style building.

When visited by the author in September 2000, Powerstock station had already been the home of Brian and Diana Read for over 30 years, named appropriately 'The Old Station'. The conservatory in the foreground was previously a milk platform. (Author)

131

Brian Read shows a 'pincher' at the former Powerstock station site, used in earlier times to move trucks when motive power was not available. Behind is the former dispatcher's hut – subsequently extended. (Author)

Apart from a temporary closure between 1917 and 1919, the West Bay extension survived until 1930. Competition from motor buses was on the increase and the resort had not developed as expected. On 22nd September 1930 passenger services were withdrawn and East Street station closed. West Bay remained open for goods traffic. The closure passed almost without notice. Within a year or so a new use for West Bay came with the arrival of numerous GWR camping coaches. For £3 per week it was possible to rent a 6-berth coach provided travel to the area was by rail.

All this changed when the Second World War came with pill boxes and tank traps soon to be erected along the line. Mobile anti-aircraft guns were mounted on railway wagons and sited in sidings provided at Bridport and Loders. The West Bay extension found a new use with train loads of shingle being

This is almost all that remains of Toller station found below a road bridge. Nearby houses are called 'Bridgend' and 'Railway Cottage'. (Author)

taken from the area to various places throughout the country for the construction of airfields. Later in the war, the coastal strip was used for practice landings from the sea by allied forces in preparation for D-Day.

After the war, the Bridport branch remained busy with 11 trains each way daily and four on Sundays. Petrol was still rationed and the motor car had not yet come to replace the trains. On 1st January 1948 the GWR became the Western Region of British Railways. The railway was no longer privately owned. A further change followed in April 1950 when regional boundary changes put the Bridport branch into the Southern Region.

On Sunday, 7th June 1958 there was a special event when West Bay station saw its first passenger train for 28 years. The occasion was organised by a railway enthusiasts' club when some 80 members toured Dorset's branch lines in a two-coach push-pull unit hauled by a Southern Railway class M7 locomotive no

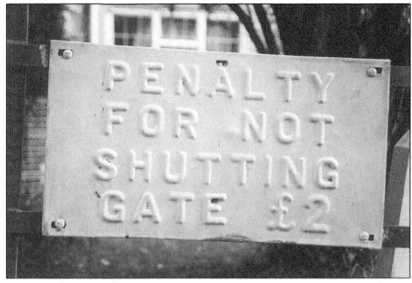

Although Toller station closed over 25 years ago, this warning notice is still fixed to an adjacent gate. (Author)

30107. Prior to travelling on the Bridport branch, the train had reached Easton on the Portland line and also the site of the original Poole station on the Hamworthy Goods branch.

Over the next few years the branch was compelled to give up many of its services. In June 1959 Bridport's engine shed closed as three-car diesel units took over the line and during 1960/1961 goods services were withdrawn from Toller and Powerstock. In its time Toller handled a considerable traffic in watercress with supplies reaching as far away as Birmingham, Leeds, Sheffield and Bolton. From the end of 1962 there were no trains on Sundays and the West Bay extension closed to what little goods traffic remained. On 25th August 1963 West Bay saw its final steam train. The Southern Counties Touring Society chartered a seven-coach train hauled by pannier tank locomotives nos 4689 and 7782 which pulled into the small terminus.

When the Beeching Plan was announced, Bridport was listed

for closure but no immediate action took place. Yet the writing was surely on the wall. In 1965 the rails of the West Bay extension (not very long since relaid!) were removed, and Bridport lost its signal box and its goods traffic when sidings were lifted. Bridport station which had at one time employed a staff of 25 was reduced to three. Eventually on 7th October 1965 British Rail announced that due to losses the branch would close on 3rd October 1966 and in its place a weekday bus service would be introduced to meet main-line trains at Maiden Newton.

In April 1966 a Public Enquiry was held chaired by Commander M.H. Pugh for the Transport Users Consultative Committee (South Eastern Area) when strong views were put forward as to why the branch should be retained. Hardship to the local residents, loss of tourist and holiday trade plus inadequate existing roads were among the points put forward

Toller, an intermediate station on the Bridport branch, viewed from the train in August 1960. Goods traffic at Toller ended in April 1960 and Toller became an unstaffed station in April 1966. (F.A.Blencowe/R.K.Blencowe)

135

but it was not until 4th June 1967 that the Minister of Transport, Mrs Barbara Castle, said that the Bridport line must stay open. Even so the downgrading went on. Such instances included the singling of the main line between Yeovil and Dorchester in 1968 and in 1969 Bridport became an unstaffed station. It seemed difficult to believe that British Rail had any intentions other than to close the branch at the earliest opportunity.

On 11th June 1971 British Rail gave notice to close the line completely and again an enquiry was held. As before valid arguments were put forward and once again a decision was deferred. It was to be almost another four years before a statement was finally made. The Secretary of State for the Environment announced that the Bridport line, Dorset's last branch line, would close on 5th May 1975. Again there was opposition but nothing could be done.

Before the last train left Maiden Newton on 3rd May for Bridport, members of the Dorset Transport Circle laid a wreath on the front of the train. As the train pulled away detonators exploded. All along the line, at Toller and Powerstock and at Bridport, crowds looked on much as they had nearly 120 years previously when the branch first came to life.

There is still much evidence of the line that closed just over 25 years ago. The track has gone at Maiden Newton but a bay can be seen. Powerstock's station building, its platform, its milk platform and dispatcher's hut are still there. The station became a private residence in the early 1970s when Brian and Diana Read took possession of the run-down building. Today much improvement and conversion have been done. Brian Read took great pride in showing the author and his wife a 'pincher' found at the site – a long and heavy metal implement used for moving trucks in a siding without motive power.

At Toller down a short track by a road bridge, the platform edge can be found. The platform and building at West Bay, used for a time as a boat yard after closure, have survived. Today the restored building serves as an Information Centre and by the platform on a short stretch of track stand two coaches – supplied by the Southern Steam Trust which supports the Swanage

Railway. There is talk locally that plans exist for a narrow gauge railway (probably 1 ft 11½ ins) to be built connecting West Bay with Bridport. But much would need to be done and finance has to be found.

Bridport station has gone but if you should happen to be shopping at the Co-op Pioneer Supermarket then you could well be standing where once local folk waited for a train!

12
A Branch Line To Lyme Regis

Axminster/Combpyne/Lyme Regis

A young family watch at Lyme Regis station, August 1960, as a passenger train headed by Adams Radial class 415, no 30584 awaits departure. (F.A.Blencowe/R.K.Blencowe)

Although new railway developments spread throughout Dorset during the latter part of the 19th century, Lyme Regis had to wait many more years before it got its own branch line. Numerous schemes involving the town came to nothing. In August 1871 the Lyme Regis Railway Company received Royal approval granting powers to connect the town with the L&SWR main line at

138

A train prepares to cross Cannington Viaduct on the Lyme Regis branch. During construction in 1903 a landslip necessitated replacement of the centre arches and the resultant unevenness can be seen in this picture. (R.K.Blencowe)

Axminster. Although nothing happened for three years, the townsfolk must have been heartened when, on 29th September 1874, a ceremony of cutting the first sod was held. The day was declared a public holiday, there were decorations in Broad Street and the bells of St Michael's church rang at intervals. For the occasion, the Mayoress, Mrs Skinner, used a spade which was duly inscribed 'Lyme Regis Railway'.

However, this optimism was premature for there was difficulty in raising capital. Although the Bill had passed through the House of Commons it was withdrawn from the Lords. Further delays allowed the powers to lapse in 1876 and Lyme Regis once again found itself without the prospect of a railway. Approaches were made to the L&SWR over the next ten years or so for backing but these were not successful. In March 1898 the

Axminster station building opened with the main line in 1860 whereas trains from Axminster to Lyme Regis did not commence until August 1903. (Author)

people of Axminster organised a petition containing 1,630 names, said to be 20 yards long, and presented it to the L&SWR directors. Promises were made but again they came to nothing.

Twenty-four years after the original sod-cutting ceremony had taken place, the line's promoters came to realise that if any railway was ever to be built, then they must organise it themselves. Help came from many quarters including a prominent landowner who lived at Rousden near Combpyne. Encouraged by such backing, application was made, through the promoters' solicitors, to the Light Railway Commissioners for an order. Success came at last on 15th June 1899 when the Axminster & Lyme Regis Light Railway was granted powers to build a line from Axminster to follow the Combpyne valley to within half a mile of Lyme Regis town centre. The L&SWR subscribed £25,000 and, on 4th April 1900, agreed to work the line.

Work to construct the line began on 19th June 1900 but unstable ground and bad weather caused delays. At Axminster the branch crossed the main line by means of a flyover to a bay platform on the up side. An intermediate station was planned at Combpyne and between Combpyne and Lyme Regis a viaduct was necessary. Named Cannington Viaduct (it was not far from Cannington Farm) this was a large ten-arch concrete structure, 182 yards long and with a maximum height of 93 ft. A 1,000 ft long aerial cable-way supported by two wooden pylons was erected to assist construction.

A Board of Trade inspection of the branch was arranged for 18th May 1903 but this had to be postponed since, after prolonged rains, a section of the viaduct had slipped. Owing

A passenger train headed by ex-L&SWR Adams class 415 no 30582 awaits departure to Lyme Regis in July 1958. (J.Champion/R.K.Blencowe)

A train arrives at Lyme Regis, July 1949. The branch suffered little from the Second World War although, as elsewhere, station nameboards were removed in case of a German invasion. (John H. Meredith)

to greensand encountered on the floor of the valley, the earth bank had tipped against the Axminster end abutment causing this and the adjacent pier to settle and the intervening arch crown to rise. Following replacement of the arch crown by a brick arch and the building of diaphragm walls to support the arch between nos 2 and 3 piers, it was agreed on 22nd August 1903 that the line could be opened. As far as the viaduct was concerned, a speed limit of 12 to 15 mph was imposed and a watchman employed to note any further serious settlement.

Opening day for the branch was 24th August 1903. The first train left Lyme Regis at 9.40 am with little celebration. By midday festivities got underway with an official party leaving Lyme Regis on the 12.25 pm train. Apart from many dignitaries and representatives involved with the construction of the line, passengers included 200 lucky school children from the area. In

An Ivatt 2MT class no 41295 waits in the Lyme Regis bay at Axminster station in the early 1960s. In the last few years of the branch's life these locomotives took over from the earlier Adams Radial tanks. (R.K.Blencowe)

all there were almost 500 passengers and to accommodate them the train comprised 13 gas-lit four-wheeled coaches hauled by two 0-6-0 Terrier tank locomotives bought especially for the line. These came from the London, Brighton & South Coast Railway (LB&SCR) where the two engines, nos 646 *Newington* and 668 *Clapham,* had been purchased for £500 each and renumbered by the L&SWR 734 and 735.

Initially there were six return trains daily but there were difficulies from the outset. Because of the many sharp curves on the line, engineers found that the Terriers' wheelbases, although small, were tending to 'spread' the gauge of the track. However, the Terriers survived until 1906/7 by which time three 0-4-4 class 02 tank locomotives had taken their place. These continued until just before the First World War but the sharp curves continued to cause heavy wear to the engines' frames and wheels as well as to the track. The solution came finally when a class 415 Adams 4-4-2 tank locomotive (built in 1885) was tried in 1913. After modification of a bogie to give greater side play, this class proved very successful and was put into service and, over the years, both passenger and freight business slowly built up.

In July 1906 the company was fully absorbed by the L&SWR which soon found it necessary to re-lay the branch's track. By 1910 over 60,000 passengers were using the line annually. Passenger traffic was given an unexpected boost in 1908 when a massive landslip took place in the cliffs south of Combpyne with the ground catching fire (because of varying amounts of oil in the soil) and burning in a spectacular way for eight months. Excursions to Combpyne were frequent and for a time the station nameboard claimed 'Combpyne for the Landslip'.

Decline of the branch first started in 1920 when a private

A passenger train leaves Combpyne not long before the branch's closure. Although situated in a remote area, the station facilities included a signal box, sidings, an engine shed and a goods shed. (R.K.Blencowe)

*Lyme Regis station in the early 1960s. After closure in November 1965 the
site became neglected. Attempts to preserve the line failed and in 1979 much of
the station's timber was removed by the Mid-Hants Railway to later be rebuilt
as part of Alresford station. (R.K.Blencowe)*

motor bus service began between Lyme Regis and Axminster via
Charmouth. Initially it ran twice weekly but within a few months
there were four buses weekly. Matters worsened the following
year when the National Omnibus & Transport Co began a
service between Axminster station and Lyme Regis. In 1923 the
L&SWR became part of the newly-formed Southern Railway.
Existing services were maintained and the branch benefited from
through coaches from Waterloo to Lyme Regis on summer
Saturdays. However, 'economies' were creeping in because in
1930 Combpyne lost its crossing loop, signal box and its
signalling. The signal box was sold to nearby Hook Farm for
agricultural purposes!

The branch suffered little from the Second World War. As
elsewhere station nameboards were removed in case of a

145

Combpyne, the only intermediate station on the Lyme Regis branch, survives as a private residence. In this picture at the former Combpyne station building, the old and the new stand together! (Author)

German invasion and with petrol rationing in existence the line benefited when bus services were withdrawn. There was little change following nationalisation in 1948 with holiday traffic tending to increase during the 1950s. Despite this, the private motor car was on the increase and Lyme Regis station was badly sited being half a mile from the town centre and some 250 ft above sea level involving quite a steep climb. As time passed, buses provided a better service and many winter trains ran almost empty.

In 1960 track improvements were carried out to ease the severe curvature after which it was possible to replace the ageing Adams 4-4-2 tanks with Ivatt class 2, 2-6-2s. When regular steam operation ceased on 4th November 1963, diesel multiple units (DMUs) were introduced but shortage of diesels meant that occasional steam push-pull sets reappeared along the line.

146

Following publication of the Beeching Report, closure of the branch was recommended although no immediate decision was taken. Economies followed with goods facilities withdrawn from Combpyne and Lyme Regis in February 1964. In August 1964 notice was given that the line would close to passengers from 30th November. An immediate outcry followed with action groups formed and a TUCC enquiry held. Then came a prolonged wait because of difficulties in organising adequate replacement bus services.

When closure finally came on 29th November 1965, many local folk and enthusiasts caught the last DMU up-train to Axminster. Along the route people turned out to 'mourn' the loss of the railway that had served them for just over 62 years. One resident whose garden backed onto the line hoisted a Union Jack which fluttered bravely in the wind.

Cannington Viaduct still spans the valley 35 years after closure of the branch. In this picture the unevenness of the line can still be determined. (Author)

147

Axminster station where the through line has been singled and the former bay platform for trains to Lyme Regis has become totally overgrown. Commuters sculptured in metal wait on the far platform for trains that do not arrive. (Author)

Two of the locomotives that served the Lyme Regis branch have survived the years. One of these is the class Al 0-6-0 Terrier tank no 735 which in 1906 was transferred from the branch to Yeovil. It had a varied career which included duties on the Isle of Wight and on Hampshire's Meon Valley line. In 1966 it was sold to a brewery to rest outside the Hayling Billy public house on Hayling Island. Today it can be found at the Isle of Wight Railway renamed *Freshwater* and renumbered 2.

Adams Radial L&SWR no 488 also saw many changes. In 1917 it was acquired by the Ministry of Munitions to serve at a salvage depot near Sittingbourne in Kent. Two years later it was sold to the East Kent Railway. By 1939 it was derelict though considered repairable by the Southern Railway which bought it for £800 in March 1946. After an extensive overhaul at Eastleigh, the Adams

148

The 1409 hrs train bound for London Waterloo stops at Axminster, September 2000. The line from Axminster to Lyme Regis closed in November 1965. (Author)

went into Southern Railway stock as no 3488, commencing service at Lyme Regis in December 1946. The branch now possessed three Adams locomotives but by the early 1960s two had to be scrapped. The third (no 30583 at nationalisation) was purchased by the Bluebell Railway in Sussex on 9th July 1961 where it is today, no 488 once again, in good working order and fully restored to its former L&SWR glory.

After closure of the branch, Lyme Regis station became negected. An attempt was made to preserve the line but this failed. The timber building suffered badly and a buddleia bush grew in the boarded up gents! In 1979 much of the station's timber was removed by the Mid-Hants Railway to be later rebuilt as part of Alresford station. Subsequently the local authority acquired the Lyme Regis site where a number of small commercial premises have been constructed. At Combpyne, anyone passing the remote spot today would little realise the private residence was once part of a station. Closer inspection shows that it's called the 'Old Station House'.

Cannington Viaduct still stands majestically across a wide valley. It receives regular inspections from the British Rail Property Board which says there are no plans in hand to consider demolition. Trains no longer make their way cautiously across the once damaged arch where today only the ghosts of the past remain. At Axminster the main line to Exeter has been reduced to a single track. The once-busy branch bay platform on the up side has become totally overgrown.

Conclusion

The decline of many of Dorset's branches began in the 1920s. Buses were able to offer a more flexible service than the trains and road haulage was on the increase. In addition the private motor car was beginning to make its presence felt. After nationalisation in 1948, the railways, still recovering from the demands of war service, were slow to meet any competition and were losing ground. Reduced revenue was leading to increased economies and then closures, with the entire pattern of inland transport gradually changing.

An early casualty was the passenger service between Weymouth, Portland and Easton. Already lightly used, it became increasingly vulnerable to bus competition and closed on 3rd March 1952. Freight traffic, mostly stone, survived another 13 years but the line was no longer used after 1965. At the end of 1952 the Abbotsbury branch, a line that had never had any prospects anyway, closed completely except for a short section at Upwey retained for freight until 1961.

In March 1963 proposals were made in a report which became popularly known as the 'Beeching Plan'. Basically the idea was to keep lines considered suitable to rail traffic and give up the remainder. It was claimed that one third of the rail system in Britain carried only 1% of the total traffic!

The resultant closure of lines over the next decade brought heavy rail losses to Dorset. Rail traffic fell dramatically with passengers and freight becoming almost completely reliant on road transport. Within about two years of the Beeching Report, lines between Salisbury and West Moors, Brockenhurst and

Broadstone Junction and also the branch to Lyme Regis had closed to passeners.

Perhaps the greatest blow came on 7th March 1966 with the loss of the Somerset & Dorset (S&D) line. A closure date had been postponed more than once in response to public pressure and when the last train eventually ran, thousands turned up to mourn the line's loss. A mass meeting of railwaymen claimed that British Rail had deliberately run down the line, to then simply claim that the line did not pay. Heartfelt were the words scrawled in the dust at a closed station, 'Sabotaged and Defeated'.

Further losses came in the 1970s. Economies failed to save the Swanage branch which closed on 3rd January 1972 and three years later on 3rd May 1975 the last train left Bridport for Maiden Newton. In the twelve years following the Beeching Plan, Dorset was reduced to two main lines. These included the Bournemouth to Weymouth route (part of the original 'Castleman's Cork-screw') and, skirting the border to the north, the Salisbury to Exeter line, chosen by the L&SWR as its main route to the west in July 1856. A further line survived, the Weymouth to Bath line via Yeovil Pen Mill, built as a broad gauge when it opened in 1857. This line has already seen many economies and one may well wonder today how long it will continue.

Dorset's railway past is far from forgotten. At Swanage, steam lives on with trains reaching Corfe Castle and Norden's Park & Ride station. Here one can relive the earlier times when steam trains puffed their way across the Isle of Purbeck. The preserved line has struggled hard since BR closure of the branch and it can well be satisfied with its progress. Much still needs to be done and such enthusiasm deserves all possible support.

What of the future for Dorset's railways? Is it possible that the ever-increasing fares will push many commuters off the trains? Rail privatisation, we were told, would give us an exciting future. Press reports tell us that 'complaints about late, cancelled and overcrowded trains have soared since the start of rail privatisation. Figures point to an alarming deterioration in services.' The Channel Tunnel, although providing rapid links with European capitals, has yet to provide high-speed trains in the UK and the tunnel still has to prove itself financially.

A further aspect of the future is the possibility that light railway schemes might return to revitalise many parts of our country. The current successes of the Docklands Light Railway, the Tyne and Wear Metro and many others have brought about a flood of applications to build new systems elsewhere. Is it possible perhaps that the Bournemouth area, which once boasted Bournemouth Central and West stations serving numerous routes, might one day benefit from its own light railway system?

A final thought comes from novelist Thomas Hardy. In his book *Jude the Obscure,* when Sue Bridehead visited Melchester (Salisbury) she told her cousin she would rather sit in the railway station than the cathedral. 'That's the centre of town life now,' she said. Today many of Dorset's towns have long since surrendered their railways to the already overcrowded roads. What sad endings to so many fine branch lines.

Heritage Railway Lines in Dorset

Swanage Railway
Station House, Swanage BH19 1HB; Tel: 01929 425800;
Website: http://www.swanagerailway.co.uk/;
Email: info@swanagerailway.co.uk
Standard guage preserved steam railway offering a variety of steam and diesel galas. The line runs from Wareham to Swanage, with stops at Norden, Corfe Castle, Harmans Cross and Herston Halt. See their website for details on fares and events.

The Shillingstone Railway Project
The Station, Shillingstone, Blandford DT11 0SA; Tel: 01258 860696;
Website: http://shillingstone-railway-project.org.uk/
Renovated station buildings with a shop, cafe, museum and model railway exhibition. You can also see the repaired platforms, signal box and platform shelter. They have ambitious plans to relay track to the main line and sidings, and to build a locomotive shed with gantry

crane. Their website is packed with information, as well as volunteering opportunities if you would like to get involved in preserving the Age of Steam in this corner of Dorset.

Opening and Final Closure Dates of Lines to Regular Passenger Traffic

Line	Opened	Final Closure
Brockenhurst/West Moors/Hamworthy	1847	1964
Poole Junction (now Hamworthy) to Poole (now Hamworthy Goods)	1847	1896
Maiden Newton/Bridport	1857	1975
Ringwood/Hurn/Christchurch	1862	1935
Poole/Broadstone/Evercreech Junction (Somerset & Dorset Joint Railway)	1863[*1]	1966
Weymouth to Portland	1865	1952
Salisbury/Fordingbridge/West Moors	1866	1964
Poole Quay branch (goods only)	1874	1960
Bridport/West Bay	1884	1930
Wareham/Corfe Castle/Swanage[*2]	1885	1972
Upwey Junction to Abbotsbury	1885	1952
Weymouth to Weymouth Quay	1889	1987
Portland to Easton	1902	1952
Axminster/Combpyne/Lyme Regis	1903	1965
Wool to Bovington Camp (military only)	1919	1928

[*1] Final completion date of Somerset & Dorset through line.
[*2] Section of line reopened by Swanage Railway on 20th April 1984.

Bibliography

In compiling *Lost Railways of Dorset* I have referred to numerous sources which include the following and which can be recommended for further reading:

Ashley, Harry *The Dorset Village Book* and *Explore Dorset* (Countryside Books)

Atthill, Robin *The Somerset & Dorset Railway* (David & Charles)

Baker, Michael *The Waterloo to Weymouth Line* (Patrick Stephens Ltd)

Body, Geoffrey *Railways of the Southern Region* and *Railways of the Western Region* (Patrick Stephens Ltd)

Dendy Marshall, C. F. (revised Kidner, R. W.) *History of the Southern Railway* (Ian Allan Ltd)

Gammel, C. J. *Southern Branch Lines* (GRQ Publications)

Glenn, David Fereday *Rail Routes in Hampshire and East Dorset* (Ian Allan Ltd)

Jackson, B. L. and Tattersall M. J. *The Bridport Branch* (Oxford Publishing Co)

Kidner, R. W. *Southern Railway Branch Lines in the Thirties* (Oakwood Press)

Lucking, J. H. *Dorset Railways* (The Dovecote Press)

Lucking, J. H. *Railways of Dorset* (The Railway Correspondence & Travel Society)

Maggs, C. *The Bath to Weymouth Line* (Oakwood Press)

Maggs, C. and Paye P. *The Sidmouth, Seaton & Lyme Regis Branches* (Oakwood Press)

Mitchell, Vic and Smith, Keith *Branch Line to Lyme Regis* and *Bournemouth to Evercreech Junction* and *Bournemouth to Weymouth* (Middleton Press)

Robertson, Kevin and Oppitz, Leslie *Hampshire Railways Remembered* (Countryside Books)

Sykes, P. J. *Swanage Railway Guide and Stock Book* (The Southern Steam Trust)

Thomas, David St John *West Country Railway History* (David & Charles)

White, H. P. *A Regional History of the Railways of Great Britain, Vol 2 Southern England* (David & Charles)

Williams, R. A. *The London & South Western Railway, Vol 1 The Formative Years, Vol 2 Growth and Consolidation* (David & Charles)

Wright, Andrew P. M. *The Swanage Branch* (Ian Allan Ltd: Railway World Special)

Also numerous editions of the *Swanage Railway Magazine*.

INDEX

157

Swanage   45, 47, 48, 81-95, 152
Swanage Railway   9-10, 82, 89,
   91-95, 129, 136
Swanage Railway Society   88-90
Sway   33, 39, 40, 43

Templecombe   11-18 *passim*, 21, 37,
   69, 70-80 *passim*
Thornford   119, 120
Thornford Bridge Halt   119
Toller   126, 128, 133, 134, 135, 136
Transport Users Consultative
   Committee (TUCC)   24, 77, 135,
   147
Trim, 'Dinky' and Leslie
   (Breamore)   60, 64
Tuckton   28

Upwey   108, 109, 111, 118, 122, 151
Upwey Junction   107-111 *passim*,
   112, 118, 119, 122
Upwey Wishing Well Halt   122

Verwood   24, 59, 60
Victoria   118
Vulcan   14

Wareham   19, 45-57 *passim*, 81-95
   passim

'Water Snake'   20
West Bay   128-137 *passim*
Westham Halt   102, 103
West Moors   19, 22, 24, 27, 37, 58-65,
   passim, 151
Weymouth   8, 9, 11, 24, 25, 32, 40,
   42, 43-44, 54, 55, 62, 96-111 *passim*,
   112-122 *passim*, 151, 152
Weymouth Harbour   11
Weymouth Harbour
   Tramway   96, 98
Weymouth Quay   96, 98-100
Weymouth & Portland
   Railway   101, 102, 103
Wilts, Somerset & Weymouth
   Railway (WS&WR)   68, 112-113,
   116, 118, 125
Wimborne   9, 19, 20, 22, 23, 25, 26,
   35, 37, 40, 42, 43, 70, 73
   Wimborne Junction   68
Wool   46, 48, 49, 50, 51, 52
Worgret   47, 48, 82, 84, 85, 87, 91
Wyke Regis   103

Yeovil   11-18 *passim*, 54, 80, 113-119
   passim, 125, 128, 136, 148
   Yeovil Junction   13, 14
   Yeovil Pen Mill   119, 152
Yetminster   113, 116, 119

Printed in Great Britain
by Amazon

16276022R00092